SPLASH

SPLASH

The Careful Parent's Guide to Teaching Swimming

Remove the Fear, Teach the Skill

Andrew Michael Jackson, W.S.I.
Andrea Siegel, PhD

Swimming Without Fear Press
New York

Thanks to all the wonderful kids and adults who volunteered for the pictures. It was a privilege and an honor to work with such great families. These parents and children have the tolerance of saints, and all pictures that show them doing something incorrectly were staged.

We'd also like to thank Harry Connor, Harry Kraker, Kara Howe-Barboza, Mary Jackson, Mary Kate Jackson, Andrew Jackson, Anne Jackson, Martin McMorrow (with special thanks for the kicking and dexterity sections), Emily Neustadt, Jennifer Bilek, Laura Greenberg, Jane Katz, Julie Murkette, Chris Simon, Karen Starr, Jacob Tanenbaum, and all the folks at St. Sebastian's Community Center in Woodside, Queens.

Almost everything in this book was learned from other people and from teachers at organizations such as the YMCA and YWCA, the Boy Scouts of America, and the American Red Cross. Thanks to them for their wonderful help. While the authors are grateful for the instructions and advice of professionals from many organizations, this is the authors' "take" on their ideas. Organizations named herein are not affiliated with this project and do not endorse it.

Swimming Without Fear Press
New York

For contact information, go to *Books in Print* at your local library.

You are responsible for the safety of your child. Nothing will "drownproof" your child.

"Of all the preschoolers who drown, 70% were in the care of one or both parents at the time of drowning and 75% were missing from sight for 5 minutes or less." Until your child is over four years old and well-trained, nothing can save your child from drowning but your attention. Up to the age of four, children can drown almost anywhere including buckets, bath tubs, backyard inflatable pools, toilets, hot tubs, pools, spas and open water. From the ages of five to fourteen, most children who drown do so in pools or open water.

These statistics are from the Orange County, California, Fire Authority: www.hyperbaric-oxygen-info.com/drowning-statistics.html

A leading cause of drowning is panicking. If you teach children the skills in this book and practice them, the children will be much more likely to use their skills with confidence instead of getting scared when they're in the water and starting to panic.

However, your constant supervision is essential.

CONTENTS

3. Safety

Preface

Mike likes to tell the following story before he starts teaching. This is for parents and not for kids.

In an infant-preschool aquatic class Mike Jackson was teaching, the parents of a six-month-old child asked Mike if all three could come into the water together. He recommended that only one parent hold the child in the beginning, however, they insisted on coming in together. Because these parents are very educated professional people, Mike was somewhat intimidated by their achievements, and allowed them both to go in. He felt that so much education would make them more responsible.

The first class was an orientation, where Mike and the parents talk about what happens during the course. These parents were too busy to attend, so they sent one of the child's grandmothers instead. She had no intention of entering the water. She told Mike that she would bring the information back to her children who would attend the next class. She apologized for their being too busy in their professions to attend. (Mike will not reveal their identities or their professions, but hopes they have time to read this book.)

At the second class, the first time in the pool, both parents arrived with their little fellow. First they argued about who would hold him as the other went in the water. All the other parents put their children in the dance position, the correct way of entering the water with an infant or toddler, and entered the water. (See the Index for more information.) Everyone was in the water and the couple were still arguing about who should hold the baby.

Then they did the one thing Mike asks all parents NOT to do. Because they held the baby incorrectly, the baby fell in the water. All the way to the bottom. Daddy was the first dropper of the baby. Mommy submerged, picked up the baby, and brought it to the surface. She held the baby in the cheek-to-cheek hug position. (See the Index for more information.) She told the baby he was alright. The baby was crying and frightened, and did not trust Daddy anymore. Mommy yelled at Daddy for being a stupid idiot. Daddy said it was her fault for not attending the orientation.

Mommy held the baby out to look at the baby's face. The baby, wet and slippery, once against fell into the water and went straight to the bottom. Mommy submerged again to get her child.

Then, Mommy and Daddy argued loudly, blaming each other, as the baby cried and now did not trust Mommy either. (The baby said to himself, "I am going to drown. Get me out of here.")

The whole class stared at them with their mouths open. Mike explained to the class that this is what you SHOULD NOT do. Parental supervision is paramount. Your baby should put his or her head underwater only when the baby is ready. Being dropped in the water is traumatic for a baby. It will take a lot of work to help him recover from this experience.

Mike told the parents that was enough for tonight. The infant had enough and they should leave the water. They could watch from the pool deck if they wanted. Because they could not stop arguing, he had to ask them to leave. They did not return for the rest of the classes.

A year later, the little fellow was over a year old now, and Mike's very educated, professional parents signed up for their second Infant Preschool Course. The little fellow had a good memory and did not want to come into the water. Mike was not surprised. They never took the class because their child refused to go in the water.

It is important that you read the book, attend an introductory class, and be ready to learn when taking a class. Even if you are an accomplished swimmer, teaching child aquatics takes some additional education. If you can't take a class, please read this book thoroughly. With the right attitude and knowledge, you can teach your child water safety and swimming skills.

We wrote this book so you can learn how to be skilled, supportive, loving teachers of water safety and swimming for your kids.

Myths About Swimming

Myth: You can drown-proof your child.
Truth: You cannot drown-proof your child. Any child swim course that says they will drown-proof your child is making a false claim. For your child's safety, your supervision at all times is best.

Myth: Don't eat an hour before swimming or you will cramp up and drown.
Truth: It's a good idea not to swim on a full stomach, because it is not a good feeling. You are sluggish and uncomfortable. It is a good idea to avoid food that might upset your stomach.

Myth: Swimming hard is good.
Truth: You should swim as comfortably as you can with the best technique. This is the safest way to swim.

Myth: Safety is all that matters.
Truth: Safety is the first priority, but fun matters a lot.

Myth: The important thing is how to use your arms and legs.
Truth: The important thing is to know how to use your arms and legs, AND to know how to breathe. You must do all three of these things to swim properly.

Myth: Sink or swim. If you throw your child in the water, they will either sink or swim. That is the way to teach your child to swim.
Truth: You will destroy your child's confidence and possibly cause your child to drown if you try this. We believe that a child benefits most from intelligent, caring, trained parents or a trained swimming instructor.

Myth: My child is too young to go into the water or learn how to swim.
Truth: From the time a child is very young, you can show him or her in the bath that water is fun. When your child has control of his or her head movements, your child is ready to begin to go into a pool with you. Even if the child is too young to swim, he or she can learn swimming readiness skills, such as kicking feet, paddling arms, and blowing bubbles. That way, when your child is ready to learn to swim, these skills will already be in place.

Myth: Some people have heavy bones that cause them to sink.
Truth: Some people are more buoyant than others. (Bones have nothing to do with it.) But, with some assistance, all people can learn to float.

Myth: If your child goes in the water in the wintertime, he or she will get sick.
Truth: Chlorinated pool water does not make your child sick. In an indoor pool, 86 degrees or warmer, it's OK to go in in wintertime. As long as you dry your child properly and cover your child when he or she leaves the pool area, your child will be fine. Of course, subjecting your child to extreme cold or heat is dangerous.

Myth: Swimming lessons should not be play.
Truth: Good swimming lessons are a combination of fun, safety, and learning. You should try to make swimming a pleasant experience.

Myth: An infant or a young child should not be submerging.
Truth: The child should not be submerged unless you are trained properly in swim instruction for children, or they are trained properly by a swim instructor.

Myth: Pools spread diseases.
Truth: If a pool is properly taken care of, it is safe to swim in. Pools are the safest place to learn to swim because they're chlorinated and filtered. We suggest having your child wear footwear around pools because of the risk of athlete's foot.

Myth: Swimming in the ocean means you are going to be attacked by a shark.
Truth: You probably have a better chance of being struck by lightning on a sunny day than being attacked by a shark. If you attend to the posted safety notices and only swim in safe areas, there is little likelihood you will be attacked by a shark. When water is very warm, near 90 degrees, when it feels like bath water, there may be stingrays. If the water is that warm, first ask the lifeguard. In any case, some experts suggest you shuffle, don't walk, in the water. That can help scare them away. We call it the stingray shuffle.

Myth: All flotation devices are safe.
Truth: They're not. Only those PFDs that are approved by the United States Coast Guard are safe. Things made of plastic—"swimmies" and tubes—are not safe and may give you a false sense of safety.

Introduction

What makes this book different from other swimming books? **We believe that the most important thing to do first is to help your child get through the fear of swimming and water.**

Everything's been tested. Our method is straightforward and effective: First remove the fear, then teach the skills. If you demonstrate everything you want your child to try, your child is more comfortable. If you break every swimming lesson down to small, manageable mini-lessons—as we do in this book—children have fun and learn much faster. If you praise your child as your child learns, you create a wonderful, confident swimmer. If you have fun, it helps your child have fun. Your child is not so afraid to take a chance because your child is safe. You earn the child's trust over time.

This book explains the steps we take to teach swimming. It's broken up into many different chapters. We start from the very beginning, even before your child goes in the water, and continue right up through teaching your child how to swim. This book is structured to make learning as safe and fun as possible. There's an easy way to look up things and find what you're looking for in the Table of Contents at the front, and in the Index at the back. Also, the teaching process goes in order. We start out with the first lesson, which involves talking with the parents about preparing their child to go to the pool. We discuss teaching children from age six months and up. We also discuss how to find a pool and how to find a good place to teach your child. There is no substitution for a swimming class with a licensed professional instructor, but this is the next best thing.

We begin with the most elementary skills for very young children (ages six months and up). The book is stocked full of information that you need to succeed in learning how to swim in a safe way and teaching your child.

There are chapters on safety and many suggestions that will help make you and your child safer in and around the water. Learning the skills to swim is not enough to be safe around the water. This book has a lot of safety information, including rescue skills and suggestions about what to do in an emergency. Learning this information will empower you not to panic in an emergency situation. Because this book is just an introduction, we strongly encourage you to continue your studies by taking a safety course with a reputable organization such as the Red Cross.

We have a three-fold approach: safety, learning, and fun. This is a book for parents, significant others, family, friends and interested adults. We use the term "parent," throughout because it's short. Please substitute whatever term you prefer.

You can also use this book to teach yourself to swim (in a supervised area). Stay in the shallow end!

This book came about because Mike, who is a Red Cross certified Water Safety Instructor and Lifeguard, wanted a reference book for parents who could not enroll their children in swim classes he teaches. Almost everything in print, until now, is geared toward the professional swim instructor. He thought people might want a book for non-professionals who want to teach swimming correctly and make it fun. Since there wasn't one, we wrote this (with help from his friends and family, which is why we use the word "we" throughout the book. Because Mike's friend Andrea is a writer and a lifeguard, he asked her to help him make his knowledge into a book).

Parents' positive, supportive attitude is essential to every lesson in this book. We deal with safety in all aquatic situations. We take it from the very beginning—from before blowing bubbles—right up to swimming.

We break everything down into small steps. This is the way Michael Jackson teaches in Queens, New York. He has been teaching this way for fifteen years, and has had good results. There are many other ways to do it. "Different strokes for different folks."

Please note that we use masculine and feminine pronouns interchangeably. All lessons are for girls *and* boys.

We Teach Safety first, and then Learn and Have Fun

Read through the lessons and safety section so you can teach safety with every lesson. In these lessons you will learn deep water confidence, buoyancy and breath control. You will learn water entry and jumping into the pool. You learn locomotion skills such as those used in the Elementary Backstroke, sculling on the back, front Crawl, long Doggy Paddle, and Breast Stroke. The child may not be able yet to coordinate arm strokes with foot motions.

You can teach a child to swim, but hiring a professional is better. The professional has the experience. However, you are better than nothing! If you do enroll your child in classes, attend the classes and learn from the instructor. And then if you go on vacation or have a backyard pool, you can do what the instructor did and know you're doing it right. The keys are practice and patience.

After this introduction, which you should read, the other parts of this book are infant/toddler aquatics, and basic learn-to-swim for children and adults (this last part is for people who can stand in the shallow end of the pool with at least their shoulders out of the water), and safety.

Commodore Longfellow, the founder of the Red Cross lifeguard program, once said, "Water can be your best friend or your worst enemy." Being safe around water can make the experience fun and friendly.

In infant/toddler aquatics, your child gets introduced to the water. You want to make his or her first experience a pleasant one. This book will show you how to make it pleasant and safe.

The basic learn-to-swim for children and adults section shows how to remove the fear of the water and teach the basic skills of swimming.

If you're an adult and you're nervous about being in the water,
take a class for yourself; or take this book, and you and a friend can teach each other.

Take a class for you: Parenting is probably the most important job you have. The more you know about swimming, the less likely your child will have a problem later on. If you are not used to the water or are afraid of the water, you should take a swimming course before teaching a child. You'll learn a lot in the course that can help your children. If you cannot get to a course, read this book.

Taking a course in cardiopulmonary resuscitation (CPR) is a good idea for any parent, even if you don't learn to swim. God forbid, for any emergency, if your child chokes, you know the Heimlich maneuver. You know how to do a stomach thrust.

We suggest that your child take a class. The first thing parents need to know about teaching children to swim is there's no substitute for your child taking a real course. **We strongly recommend that you enroll your child in a certified recognized program—such as the Infant Preschool Aquatic Program (IPAP) in the American Red Cross swim program—so that your child can learn to swim from trained professionals. Almost everything a child needs to learn about swimming from infancy to age four is in the IPAP.**

If you're going to put your child in a course, putting him in the proper course is so important. Don't put him in something more advanced than what he's ready for. Even though it may be the "only opening," it may not be right for your child. Your child will learn, but he will also get frustrated. Try to put your child in the proper place for *his* level of development, not where you think he *should* be.

The Red Cross and the YMCA, for example, offer several levels of swimming instruction. These levels are important. Again, make sure you put your child in the appropriate level for his skills.

The idea is to enjoy the journey, not the destination. Teaching children to be safe around water is no easy task. It takes time and patience. The time you share in the water with your child is a very special time. Try to treasure every moment. This could be as much fun for you as it is for your child. It should not feel tedious. You are helping to give the gift of love of the water to your child. It will be a positive experience your child will remember for the rest of his life.

You also get peace of mind when you teach your child water safety. As Socrates allegedly said, "Everyone should know three things: How to read, write, and swim!"

All the important safety rules can be learned at a very young age. The sooner the better! We try to present many aspects of water safety. Not only will your child learn things, but so will you. Teaching your child to love the water and be safe around the water makes you feel like the best parent in the world. The more you know, the safer you are and the safer your children are.

Enjoying the Moment

The experience of being in the water with your child is a very special time to share with one another. By this we mean the water is different, enjoyable, and fun. Children have fantasies about playing with water. It intrigues them. Watching them play in the water is magical.

Teaching your child the basics of water safety and swimming is another way to build trust in your relationship with your child. Your child's trust is something you have to earn. You gradually earn this trust by not frightening your child and by allowing your child to have fun in the water.

As your child's water experience grows from exploration to actual swimming skills, your child will remember these moments. Later on in life your child will tell you how much fun he or she had. Swimming is a sport the whole family can participate in. It doesn't matter if you're good or not good, you can all get in the water. And you can all do something in the water. Even if you just splash each other, it's fun.

Mike remembers holding his very young children in the dance position and spinning in a circle. He would just watch the smile and laughter on his child's face. He says, "The next time I believe that my daughters will dance with me is at their weddings and I hope the experience will be similar."

Even though all of Mike's kids are grown up now, they still reminisce about early experiences they had in the water. When they were little, and still not very good swimmers, Mike and the children would go to the pool and play a game they called, "The Jump-In Game." The kids would stand at the edge of the pool with their toes over the edge, look at Mike in the water, and he would tell them a certain type of jump to do. For example, the "Statue of Liberty" jump, meant they would have to jump in while posing like the Statue of Liberty. Mike would be creative with his suggestions and the kids were creative with their jumps. They would not do the same old "cannon ball" but rather jumps like "The man riding a motorcycle," "The man sitting in his chair reading his paper," or the famous "Mary Poppins with the umbrella." Mike would catch them after they jumped in and help them back to the wall. **By the way, always jump feet first.** For more information about jumping in, see the Index.

These girls are about ten years old and they are on the swim team.
Here they're showing some of the jumps that Mike used to do with his kids.
Play with these jumps after your child has learned every skill in this book.

The Ballerina

Teacher, call on me!

Synchronized Swimming

Jumping Rope

Statue of Liberty

A Man Sitting in a Chair
Reading a Newspaper

If your child has fear, it's important to compare in your mind your child's fear with something you are afraid of. For example, you may fear jumping out of a plane without a parachute. This should give you a better understanding of the fear your child will feel before he or she goes in the water.

This is true of some children, not all. **A child with no fear of the water can create other problems,** such as your child jumping into the water while you're not looking, your child not listening while playing in the water, or your child thinking the water is safe when it isn't.

If the parent fears the water, this will inhibit the learning process. The child will know the parent is afraid, and therefore the child will be afraid. If you, the adult, are afraid, take a course in swimming before your child is ready. You must have confidence in the water so that you can teach your child not to be afraid. We recommend that you only teach your child how to swim in a supervised pool where you feel confident yourself. Only then will you be ready to decrease your child's fear of the water. Later in the book, we explain specific techniques to help your child get over fear of the water.

A lot of learning to swim is acclimation and adjusting. In every lesson, we address the fears children typically have about this lesson, and what you can do to help your child learn with confidence and fun. Once the child has confidence and has fun in the water, the child wants to learn, and learns very quickly. The more he or she trusts you, the easier the learning experience will be. Go slow and take your time. You work on it. Here is a theory about fear and learning:

If you take a fearful child or a fearful adult into the water and demonstrate how to breathe and use your arms and legs, and then expect the person to perform, missing a breath of air can cause him or her to panic and be at risk of drowning ...especially if you have moved into deeper water. If you work on fear first, help get a person comfortable and confident in the water, so the person feels safe; then he or she is ready to learn, and you can start to introduce different skills.

Be attentive to your child. Children show anxiety in many ways:
- Making up excuses
- Huddling or hunching up around the shoulders
- Repeatedly wiping the face to remove hair from the eyes
- Holding the body rigid
- Flinching
- Biting the lip
- Shivering (Some children are going to shiver no matter what the water temperature is. That's OK. But shivering can also be a sign of anxiety.)
- Grasping the instructor or parent, especially during flotation and submerging
- Performing strokes too short, too shallow, or too rigid
- And others...

You want the child to relax. That takes your gradually teaching him or her to be comfortable in water, and trust, which comes with time. You have to be patient. Don't get discouraged. You earn your child's trust as you teach. This is a long process but a worthwhile one. A child can't learn to swim until he or she is ready, both physically and mentally, but the child can learn swimming readiness skills, so that when the child is ready, it's easy because the child already has the skill. If your child has a strong desire to swim, your child will learn. Like learning how to juggle, learning how to swim takes dexterity. In the case of swimming, you have to know how to kick, move your arms and breathe—all together. It takes many hours of practice.

Always talk your child through something before you do it, so the child knows what's going to happen. As scary as the new skill might be, it's better to let your child know what's coming than to try to trick the child.

If something happens that terrifies your child, take the child out of the water. They always say, "If you fall off a horse, get right back on." That isn't true for swimming. Get out of the water, take a little rest, let the child know what happened. Talk your child through it.

Don't compare. Your child is unique. Every child is an individual and learns at his or her own pace. We are not early childhood education experts; this book comes from Mike's experience as a swim instructor. From what we've seen, every child is an individual. Let each child go at his or her own pace.

Don't be a jealous parent and compare your child to other children.
All children develop at their own speed.

Praise your child if he or she makes any effort at all. "You're doing a wonderful job." It's more important that the child is having fun. And if you can add in learning to having fun, you've got magic. And if you can enjoy it, you've got special magic.

Praise your child. There is no name-calling in good swim instruction. Be sensitive to your child's limitations and fears. Remember: when you're afraid of something, the fear is real. When you're not afraid—as you probably aren't afraid of water—you have to imagine what it's like to be afraid, and then you can appreciate your child's point of view.

You may not realize it when your child is taking a chance. A child may think it's scary to put his or her face in the water, to take his or her feet off the bottom of the pool, or to let go of the edge of the pool.

No matter how small your child's achievements, even if there isn't achievement, you want to give positive feedback. It makes the child want to come back next time. In each lesson we include new words for your "positive feedback collection," so you'll have new ways to encourage your child. Children want to please their parents. If you're praising your child, your child knows you're pleased with him or her.

To the parents: Do not criticize. Positive feedback, no matter what! Negative feedback does not help. Positive feedback helps. This is really important. No matter what your child does, raise your voice at your child in the water only if the child is putting his or her life or someone else's life at risk. If your child makes a "mistake," it's not a mistake. Remember, your child is learning. From personal experience, we know we don't learn anything the first time. Sometimes we've got to make the same mistake many, many times.

With swimming, sometimes you've got to learn the wrong way before you learn the right way. If you're able to motivate your child to get from one side of the pool to the other in an unorthodox way, that's still swimming. One of the good parts of teaching children is as they swim better, they get more relaxed, and their strokes improve, especially with instruction. Positive reinforcement of what they're doing is important.

About special needs children

Water can be wonderful for children with special needs. You may not need a special teacher, but you must ask your doctor before taking your child into the water. We have seen children from all different places on the autism spectrum, children with Down's Syndrome, children with ADHD, children with Sensory Perception Disorder, children with Polio, children with birth defects, children with Multiple Sclerosis, and many other issues learn to have fun in the water, learn to swim, and in many cases, gain a lot from the experience.

Keep an even temper. Some people get annoyed too often. They try to push their child to keep up with the other children. You can slow down the learning process if you scare your child or if your child is not having fun. Your child won't want to come back. And when your child doesn't come back, your child loses the opportunity to learn water skills.

In the beginning, especially for the younger ones, being in the water has to be more fun than learning. You add the learning as you go along. When, later, you're teaching them swimming, there'll be more learning, and then a little bit of fun at the end. You have to have balance, and mix it all together. One way to keep an even temper is to take a break, get a drink of water, or sit in the shade for a while. We don't want to start getting spiritual here, but if you are the praying type and you have trouble keeping your temper, try a spiritual approach. Also, if you're the wrong parent to do the job, have the other parent do it. Only work for short amounts of time, and break the teaching down into tiny steps.

On a basic level: it's ok for the child to stay out of the water. If the child wants to play on the deck, play with the child there. If you pull the child in, the next time you go to the pool, your child will think, "Oh, Daddy pulled me into the water. I don't want to go."

If the child doesn't want to go into the pool, it's alright. Put the Personal Flotation Device (PFD) on the child and sit the child in the stands, or on a towel near the pool. Swim around and have fun (while keeping an eye on your child). Be a powerful example. Your child says, "Boy, Dad's having fun. Mom's having fun. Maybe I should go in there." Or go to a pool when other children are there having fun. When your child sees other children enjoying themselves, your child will want to enter the water.

If you live in a cold climate, you may only have the summertime. If you're not near a pool, you may only be able to teach swimming when you're on vacation. But when you do have time, you can do so much in a few weeks. You can make real progress.

When you're looking for a good place for your child to learn

Once you learn to swim, other bodies of water can be great. Details are below. Pools that are filtered with chlorinated water, salt water or other types of pool sanitizing solutions are the best places to teach your child to swim. Look for a quiet uncrowded swimming pool where you can see the bottom.

Vary the lessons. This is very important. Children get bored even if they're doing something well. After a few minutes—the time depends on the attention span of the child—change to a new activity. Do an activity for up to ten minutes. Change activities BEFORE the child gets frustrated. Change the activity even when it's going well. Children love to show their parents what they can do. "Look at me, Mom!" To help the child learn more, praise the child and suggest other options. "That's good! Now try this!"

For example, if you're teaching your child to move his or her arms and the child is not getting it or doesn't seem to be having fun doing it, move on to blowing bubbles.

There's always something else you can try: from learning how to blow a ping-pong ball across the surface of the water, to blowing bubbles in the water, to paddling your arms underwater like a Doggy Paddle, to kicking your feet. Also, you could try floating and jellyfish floating and the Elementary Backstroke (see the Index for more information.)

Ten minutes is a long time to do one thing. Unless your child seems really interested and eager and excited to get it, move on to something else, and then come back later. This way the child doesn't get bored. It's important to jump from one thing to another. Kids get bored. You want to constantly challenge their interest. At the same time, kids learn through repetition and practice. Be prepared to do things over and over until your child is comfortable. At the end of each lesson we play games in the water for fifteen minutes. We make it fun so the kids want to come back.

If you know there's something your child does not like, you can sandwich it between two things the child likes to do.

Some kids do great on the breaststroke. They're natural.

We say, "How come all of a sudden you're swimming?"

"Well, I never did this stroke before, and I like this stroke."

You demonstrate everything. Your child does not have to do everything you demonstrate for them. Sometimes your child won't want to try a skill while you're looking—he or she is afraid of failure or might just want to practice independently and show you later. Respect that possibility, and move on to the next skill.

Start at home. Talk up swimming at home. Start the lessons at home (see the Index under "Starting" for lessons that can be learned before your child goes in a pool.) When we give an Infant Preschool Aquatic Program (IPAP) class, the class is only a half-hour each time, and the class runs eight sessions. So, it's really only four hours in the water. If you go on vacation, you could be in and out of the water all day. You can do a lot of things in a short period of time.

If you're landlocked, and don't live near a pool, you can always go over pool rules. This can help. Maybe your child goes on vacation with a friend, and you're not there to watch, but he already knows not to go in the water alone. He already knows to have a buddy, to swim in a supervised area, not to swim if the water feels really cold. He knows not to go in if the water is dirty. You can help your child by teaching these things. (See the Safety section in the Index for more information.)

**If your child can do a lesson or a skill without thinking about it,
the child is ready for the next step.**

Review. Always review the basics with your child each time you get in the water. Children tend to forget. Even if your child learned a skill a month ago, he or she may forget it this time. If, for example, you're teaching arm movements, be sure to say, "Remember how we kicked our feet last time?" And practice a little what you did last time. "We all forget to point our toes when kicking. Kick gently. Don't kick too hard. Keep your hands flat and open." It comes right back, but we need reminders.

Plan. Think about what you want to do in the pool before each lesson. Have an idea of a lesson plan. Be flexible. If your plan doesn't seem to be working—and they often don't—try something else.

Review Some More:
- Supervise your child.
- Go easy. Don't push.
- Your child is unique. Don't compare.

Prepare and then execute: Prepare at home and then try to stick to your plan at the pool. You may not be able to, but it is easier to work from a plan.
- Refer to the book.
- Try it yourself first. It's easier to explain if you know what it feels like.
- Give your child positive feedback.
- Ask swim teachers and lifeguards questions.
- Remember: your purpose is to have fun.

The principles of learning. Children tend to repeat pleasant things, and not repeat unpleasant ones, so you have to make the learning process fun. Children will perform a task when they're physiologically and psychologically ready to do so, not before. Repetitiveness is necessary to master a skill. Again, like with juggling, you have to practice.

Thorndike's Laws of Learning

"Learning depends on three principles: the laws of effect, readiness, and frequency."

1. EFFECT: "A learner tends to repeat those things that are pleasing on not to repeat those things that are displeasing,"

2. READINESS: "Individuals perform a task when they are ready, both physically and psychologically, to perform,"

3. FREQUENCY: "Learning requires repetition for the skill to be mastered."

— Edward Thorndike, Learning Theorist
from the *American Red Cross Water Safety Instructor's Manual* (page 29)

Age ranges and what to expect

At what age can a child learn swimming readiness skills? Some Australian instructors teach newborns. Americans often like to wait until after the child can control his or her head. We're going with the Americans on this. (Also, you are *never* too old to learn to swim.)

Familiarize your child with the water. This could start with bathing time. Long before we go into a pool, we're bathing the child. We can start acclimating children to the water during the bath. Let your child know the water is fun by singing in the tub, putting water over your head and your child's, and enjoying it yourself.

While you and your child are bonding, having fun, and exploring the aquatic experience, this book will help you set goals that you can work towards for different age groups and different stages. The purpose of these activities is to give a safe and positive experience for you and your child which will give your child a good foundation in learning swimming readiness skills.

Initially, we're teaching proper handling of the child, safely entering and leaving the water, and acclimating children to the water so they don't fear it.

The early lessons are for anyone getting acquainted with the water, including preschoolers, toddlers, and infants. The American Red Cross IPAP suggests that a child be 6 months old before going into the water, or a child can start as soon as the child can hold up his or her own head.

At seven months old, many children can recognize the word "No." You can start teaching water safety skills, as in, "No. Don't go in the water without an adult."

For children up to 24 months, the parent must hold the child in the water. Children up to 36 months old should not be left alone in the water, even with a Coast Guard approved flotation device on them. A scare can cause the child to have a big setback. Always supervise your children in or near water.

Up to 3 years old, parents should only expect to have fun and help the child get acclimated to the water. Your knowledge of how to hold and support your child is paramount for the child's safety. Remember, the purpose of bringing your child into the water so young is to have positive experiences in the water very early. Get your child comfortable with the water as soon as possible. (More about this is detailed later in the specific lessons.) However, adults can start passing the child back and forth between them, holding the child securely. The parent can also start training the child to move away, using buoys, kick boards, swim bars, and even those low-cost plactic swim "noodles." Children start to experience their own natural buoyancy.

Very few children learn to float early on, but parents learn how to teach it to be ready for when the children are ready. You can start explaining safety things to children at any age. Sometimes at around two, they may start to understand. You can do it with songs and stories. Be creative. When you tell them about not crossing the street, also tell them never to go in the water without a lifeguard. Tell them about the deep end, and about never diving in, and about always having a buddy with you. Tell them you never swim alone.

As the child continues to grow, the child becomes ready for the more challenging skills. Later lessons described in this book (see the Index under "Teaching swimming readiness skills") focus just on the abilities of preschoolers and older people, since they have developed enough physically to learn these skills. Children develop the necessary dexterity at different times. These skills prepare them later to be "on their own" in the water, with the parents supervising AT ALL TIMES.

For preschoolers between the ages of three and five, if the child can stand with his or her head above water, the parent must supervise at all times. At this age, unless the child has a PFD on, the parent should be in the water. You don't want to miss out on the fun. If your child can stand and is comfortable in the water, the child is ready to learn swimming readiness skills. You'll read more about this later in the book.

Children over the age of five often start to get the dexterity to swim. This depends on many factors including the child's height (whether the child can stand in the pool with his or her head above water), coordination, buoyancy, and also the child's fear of the water. It also depends on the amount of time the child has practiced. When you're swimming, it's as complicated as juggling. You have to be able to breathe, move your arms and your legs all in a pattern. And you're not really swimming until you do that. That requires a certain level of physical development. You can't rush nature. If your child isn't yet at that level, your child may be able to get two or three feet into the water in a jump and go like heck, but unless he or she has the swimming skills, the child's head is going to go underwater, and the child will panic.

We don't know if this is because of how nature works, or how kids are nurtured, but we've observed that girls can have swimming dexterity faster than boys of the same age. Again, every child is unique.

~~ SPLASH ~~

PART II
For infants, toddlers (and older people…)

Before or after you have a baby, and you're thinking about swimming lessons: New parents have many things to think about. Here's one of them: One of the most important things you can give your child is the love of the water. If you are a non-swimmer or have fear of the water, it will be hard for you to teach someone to swim.

If you fear the water, take some swimming lessons so you don't transfer the fear to your child. Don't be afraid of signing up for a swimming class. It can be both beneficial and fun.

If you, the adult, are an excellent swimmer, for example a competitive swimmer, a trained lifeguard, or an advanced swimmer, this is not enough knowledge to allow you to teach the elementary skills effectively and efficiently. Even if you're the best swimmer in the world, it doesn't mean you can teach children to swim. That's a different kind of swimming skill. This book gives you the ability to start from the very beginning.

For all parents. This book teaches the skills you need for your children to be safe in and around the water. *If you do not think these are important skills to give your child, this may not be the book for you.* If you want to give your child as many skills in life as possible, then this is the book for you, because swimming is one of the most important skills your child will ever learn.

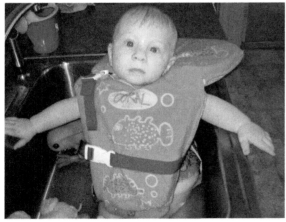

Even before you take them to the pool, try the PFD at home. Let them wear the PFD in the bathtub, or bathing in the sink, as you see here. You want the child to get comfortable wearing the PFD.

The transition of going to a pool for the first time and having to wear a PFD is difficult. If the child is comfortable with a PFD, that makes the transition easier. This is a Coast Guard approved #3 PFD. It's made for child who is more familiar with the water and weighs over 50 pounds.

Preparation: Months before you take your child to the pool, **start talking** with your child in a positive way about the water. Tell you child how much fun it's going to be. You can also tell your child about rules and regulations. If the facility you'll be using requires that you wear bathing caps, have your child **practice wearing the swim cap** at home so your child will feel comfortable when he or she has to wear it in the water. You can call your child's cap a "fun hat" and buy it in a the child's favorite color so your child will be more willing to wear it. You can also demonstrate by wearing your cap. Make everything fun. Also, as we have mentioned before, have your child **practice wearing the PFD** around the house so your child gets comfortable with how it feels.

Ask your neighbors and other parents about pools in the area. Important questions are: Do they teach swimming there? You're looking for a place with experience teaching swimming with professional, certified water safety instructors. How many kids are in the class? Optimal size is 15 or fewer students. There should also be a lifeguard present. What is the age range of the kids? Look for teachers with experience teaching kids your child's age and level of experience. Talk to people who have gone through the program and get their advice. What is the cost? It varies. What do they recommend and why? Is it a Red Cross approved or a YMCA "Mommy and Me" or is it their own program?

Go to the Facility: There are two reasons to take a look at swimming facilities. The first reason is for you: you can find out where the best facilities are in your area, and see for yourself what makes a good swimming facility. The second reason is to take your child to the facility so he or she can be familiar and comfortable with it before even going in the water. Let your child see it for him or herself. If you're going to sign your child up for a swim program, go with your child at a time when other children are taking lessons in the water.

In any event, **try going during the kids' swim time** so your child will see other children having fun in the water. Remember to point out the deep end, the shallow end, the rules about not running around the pool, and to introduce your child to the lifeguard so your child feels that the lifeguard is a friend. Make it sound like fun, and make sure you enjoy yourself. Remember, if you're confident and having fun, so is your child. Make the first experience a pleasant one. Don't get discouraged: this may take a little patience. If you see a friend, a neighbor, or someone your child knows from school, point this out to your child. It lets your child relate better because someone he or she knows is enjoying the water.

Find out more. Here are some question to ask and things to look into:

1. Does the facility teach swimming? If so, we suggest you enroll your child in a course.

2. Are the swim instructors certified by the Red Cross, or some other well-respected certifying group?

3. How deep is the water? With an infant, always hold the child, so the depth of water does not matter except as it's comfortable for you. The shallower the depth in the low end, the easier it is to teach. For toddlers and preschoolers, look for a facility that's set up for small children, a kiddie pool or a pool where there's a platform or a shallow end that makes the floor less than two feet deep so your child's feet can touch the bottom. That makes it easier to teach your child. It also makes your child feel safer.

4. If you are going to use this book to teach on your own, look to see if there is a large staircase. A staircase can be a place that makes the kids feel secure while they're learning. The staircase is a place to teach younger and small children individual skills. They can sit, can learn to move their arms, blow bubbles, kick their feet and put their face in the water.

5. Are lifeguards on duty at all times?

6. What's the temperature of the water? The temperature should be around 86°. That's a perfect temperature for teaching, but most pools are going to be cooler than that. See the information in the safety section on hot and cold in the Index for more information.

7. Look and see: Does the pool look clean? Make sure it is a clean and safe environment.

8. Chlorination. Outdoor pools can change really fast. If, after swimming, your skin is slippery and your eyes are burning, talk to the management. They may be over-chlorinating the pool, or it may not have the right pH.

9. What hours can the pool be used? Make sure the hours are convenient for you. It's good to join a pool and then be able to use it because it's open when you're available.

10. Are family times and high school times separate? If not, during that time, is an area sectioned off for non-swimming activities?

11. Look at the rules about safety. They should be posted. They change from facility to facility.

12. Part of the shallow end should be sectioned off so you don't interfere with other swimmers while you're in the water with your child.

13. Look at the types of devices they have for getting in and out of the pool. Keep in mind that a staircase is easier than a ladder if you're holding a small child. We do not recommend joining a pool that only has a ladder. Make sure the pool has a staircase.

14. It is important to feel safe and comfortable.

See the Index under Safety for information about different types of swim facilities. Also see the Index under Safety for information about water temperature and safety.

On your first trip into the water. If your child is unhappy, don't push. Take your child out of the pool and warm him or her up. You two can sit and watch other kids in the pool. You can sit on the pool step and maybe put your feet in the water. Wait until you've visited the pool three times more to go back in the water. Each time you go, always make an attempt to go in the water. The only time we insist on going in the water is the third attempt. We let the child cry for five or ten minutes if he or she doesn't cheer up. And then we take the child out. This is a de-sensitization process. See the Index under Starting for more information about talking up going to the pool. Visit the pool. Talk about it. Make it something to look forward to.

Let your child play with the toys that we'll later use to learn with. Then the toys will be familiar to the child when he or she starts learning with them.

Once the baby is in the water and starting to enjoy it, just have fun.

Walk around holding the baby close and let her or him enjoy the water. Now, remember: if you're having fun, the baby's having fun.

Some pool toys are good for playing and some are good for learning. We're not ready to teach yet. Let your child play with the toys and have fun.

Try pool toys. Sometimes the simplest toy is the best. A ping-pong ball can work miracles. Play with pool toys at home and then bring them to the pool.

Act as if the water temperature is perfect, but if your child gets cold, take her or him out of the pool. Wrap the child up in a towel and warm him or her up. Even take the child to the showers and give him or her a warm shower. It's hard for a child to learn if the child is cold.

Act as if the water is a fine temperature. You won't find a pool that's human body temperature, 98.6°. The warmest pools you'll find are about 90°, and they're usually used for therapy. Pools at that temperature feel like bath water. The pool we use here in Queens is about 84°, which is cool. This is because a lot of people use the pool for swimming, exercise, and swimming teams, so they keep it cooler. For an infant/toddler or pre-school class, it's not ideal. It should be a little warmer. The ideal temperature for teaching is about 86°. Most pools used for swimming, which are often also used for teaching, are about 82° or 83°. That's good for swimming, but you need to be aware of your child showing signs of being cold.

As you get in the water while holding your child, say, "Oh the water is very comfortable today. It feels good. It's just like the bathtub at home." Keep your feelings to yourself.

It's important to use good sense. If you, the adult, get in the water and make a fuss, "Oh man, it's cold!", your kid is going to be cold. When you get in, even though you feel cold, act as if, "Oh, it's very nice today! It's fun!" Even though the child feels cold at first, as you did, you didn't give the child the impression that you're cold. The child is going to want to emulate you. It's easier for an adult to understand that the water starts to feel warmer when you move around in it. But it's your responsibility to know when the water really is cold—when you see your child shivering or the child's lips turning blue, get him or her out of the water. Take a break, go take a warm shower, and wrap the child in a towel.

Remember: the child is warmer in the water than when he or she gets out. If you notice your child is cold and you take the child out, then you let the child sit (without wrapping the child in a dry towel) on the side

Unhappy Baby. The baby's too young to be unhappy. You want to make this a pleasant experience. When the baby's making this face, it should only be in an emergency.

I'm not sure if I'm happy yet.

Now I'm happy.

of the pool, the water on the child's body is going to evaporate and he or she is actually going to get colder. Evaporation cools the body more. So if you're only going to stay at the pool a short time longer, leave her or him in the water until you're finished.

More and more children are taking classes while wearing specially designed shirts that help keep them warm. If you're interested in this product, go to your local sporting goods store for more information.

To keep your infant warm:

- Hold the child close to your body. The child will absorb some of your warmth.
- When the infant gets wet, keep her or him wet until you are ready to get out. This means once the baby gets wet up to the shoulders, keep the shoulders in the water. If you lift the child out, the water will evaporate off the child's body, and that will make her or him colder.
- If the baby wears a T-shirt in the water, it may reduce heat loss (it also provides some sun protection).

First Lesson
Introducing water to the face

In the beginning it may not start off as wonderfully as you think it should. It may take some patience and time before the child learns a skill. If the child does not like what you are teaching, stop and do something else.

Introducing water to the face: Squeeze a sponge in the bathtub.

This is the first lesson. Getting your face wet is the beginning of putting your face

When introducing water to the child's face, you put a few drops on your face first. If the child is old enough, the child can put a few drops on your face.

Then you introduce a few drops of water to your child's face. This is something you can practice at home in the tub.

in the water. All good swimmers put their faces in the water.

Introducing water to the face occurs at home while giving your child a bath. Start when you are washing your child's face. Use a clean washrag or sponge with no soap in it. You can also use a small toy watering can. You can pour it out, and say, "This is how we water flowers and make them grow. And this is how we water children and make them grow." Allow a few drips to go on the baby's head. Let a little bit of water roll down the baby's face. Three things can happen: 1) Baby might like it. 2) Baby may not do anything. 3) Baby may not like it.

1. **Baby likes it**. If the baby likes it, continue and use a little more water at each bath time. Remember to take your time. It all doesn't have to be done in one bath. You should do this over a series of many baths. Remember always give positive feedback, "You're doing beautifully." "How wonderful, you like the water." Babies love to hear the tone of voice of parents saying good things to them.

2. **Baby does not do anything**. The baby may not do anything. Just go slow. Try not to scare the baby. Use those kind words: "My little Esther Williams." "My little Jane Katz." "What a wonderful swimmer you'll be."

3. **Baby does not like it.** If the baby cries or is frightened by water on the face, slow down and next time just have the water go down the sides of the baby's head, a few drops at a time. Try not to get it in the baby's eyes. If this fails, take the bath with the child. Dribble water over your head. This will allow the baby to see water go over your head and in your face. The baby will see how fun it is for you, and then will want to do it. Your job is to say, "Weeeee," when the water is going over your face so it looks like you're having fun. You can also try singing the Baby Beluga song. (See the Index under Songs for more information.)

The water should be lukewarm. This should be done *before* washing the baby. We want the baby to have a good experience. If there is soap in the water, or if there is already shampoo on the child's head, the water may burn the baby's eyes.

Make sure your child does not drink the water as it comes down his or her face. Sometimes your child might want to lap it like a puppy dog would. It's not a good habit to get into for swimming.

This is the beginning of the child putting his or her face in the water. However, actually putting the face in the water is a very advanced skill that we will teach in another part of the book. Remember that every skill we teach in the beginning is an elementary skill, moving in the direction of a more advanced skill that will bring us closer to swimming, our ultimate goal.

Again, remember to take your time and not to rush. This is a slow process.

Holding an Infant In and Out of the Pool: The Dance Position

This is a good way to enter the water. She's holding the rail in one hand. She's holding him securely in the dance position—she has her arm around his back. One of his legs is in the front of her hip and the other is behind. So, he's sitting very comfortably on her hip. Entering the water backwards is safer. It is the recommended way to enter the water by stairs. If you have an above-ground or in-ground pool at home, you can only use the dance position on a ladder that is slanted at a 45° angle, or on a staircase. If it's a vertical ladder, don't use the dance position. See the next photo series for other entry options.

Before your child enters the pool, there are some things for you to learn. The first position parents have to learn is called the "dance position" or the "carrying hold." This should be used with infants who are old enough to have control of their heads but they do not have to be able to to sit or stand on their own. This means the child needs your support.

After your child can hold his or her head up, and can look left or right when you call the child's name, you can consider beginning to familiarize your child with being in a swimming pool. You have to be able to pick up the child without having to support his or her head. Six months old is often a safe age. It's the youngest age recommended by the American Red Cross for starting to learn. A child this age is not going to learn to swim. You and your child are going to start to enjoy the water together.

In this position, you put the baby on or above your hip with one of the baby's legs in front of your hip and one in back of your hip. Use your arm closest to the baby by putting your arm on the infant's back. DO NOT put your arm under the baby's bottom, because if the baby doesn't want to be held, she or he will arch back or go limp, and you're liable to lose the child.

This is an older child, but no matter how old your child is, your wearing a T-shirt may help your child feel more secure. Also, children can grab your swim suit and pull on your straps. Wearing a T-shirt prevents that.

With your free hand, you can hold the baby's free hand. (This simulates a dance position, hence the name of the hold.) What's good about this position is that you can let go of the baby's hand with your opposite hand and have that hand free to do other things. You will need that free hand to hold a banister as you enter and exit the water. You can also use it to pick up things, etc. This hold makes the baby feel secure and is a safe method for moving the baby around in the water.

In the beginning, the child may hold on to you tightly, and that's fine. You can hold the baby as tightly as you like. If you wear a T-shirt in the water, the baby can get a better grip on you. The child is getting adjusted to the water. Gradually he or she will learn not to hold on so tight, and to use his or her own buoyancy to feel free and comfortable in the water.

Adult entries into and exits from the water

There are proven safe ways of entering and exiting the pool with an infant or small child.

You need one set of skills for infants who can't yet walk or sit on their own. You need a different set of skills for children approximately one year old and up (see the Index for the section on Teaching Swimming Readiness Skills for more information).

Anywhere around a pool, it can be wet and very slippery. Use caution at all times. Look at the pool and see what kinds of ladders or stairs they have. When you're involved with educating a child, using a pool with stairs that gradually go down into the shallow end is the easiest way to get into a pool. Next in difficulty is an "ease-in" entry, which means you sit at the edge of the pool on the shallow end and gradually lower yourself in the water. The least preferable way to let yourself into the water is using a ladder.

For people who can swim, a safer way to get in the water without jumping in.

Ease-in entry.
Let someone else hold your child. Sit at the side of the shallow end. Put your hands beside your hips and hold the edge of the pool. Wiggle back and forth toward the edge of pool on your rear end.

As your bottom drops off the edge of the pool, catch your weight on your arms, and slowly lower yourself into the water.

As your feet touch the bottom, you can let go of the wall.

Now you're in, nice and safe.

EASE-IN ENTRY

You need to learn this because it is something you will later show your child how to do. If you know what it feels like, you will be a better teacher.

While you are doing the ease-in entry, have someone else hold or watch your child. You can also place the child on the edge of the pool on a blanket, towel or changing mat. Put one arm between the child and the pool so the child can't roll into the pool. Once you're in, pick up your child and put him or her in the dance position.

1. Sit at the side of the shallow end.

2. Put your hands beside your hips and hold the edge of the pool.

3. Wiggle back and forth forward toward the lip of the pool, making believe you are walking using the cheeks of your buttocks.

4. When your bottom drops off the edge of the pool, your weight will transfer from your bottom to your arms. Slowly bend your elbows, lowering your body into the water until your feet touch bottom. Release the pool edge when it feels right.

When you get in and out of the water holding a small child, you only have one arm to secure your balance. You must go slowly and take precautions. **Many accidents happen when a small child is dropped or wiggles himself or herself free from the parent's grip.** This can be a big setback in the learning process, creating a fear in your child that can take a long time to overcome. The fear makes it much more difficult to give your child a pleasant experience around the water. We try to avoid this setback by having a secure hold on the child and by remembering how important it is to keep your child's head above water. Also, we do not want you to get hurt.

Sometimes your child wriggles in your arms in the water and it's hard to hold on. If this happens to you, and you drop your child, comfort and calm your child, then talk through what happened with her or him:

"Your head went underwater, but nothing bad happened. And I am here for you." Take responsibility: "It was my fault that happened. I wasn't watching..." Or "I stepped on a..." Or "I slipped." Tell your child the truth.

It's like dropping your kid at home. You don't mean to do it. It happens.

If you have a child who is very active and who will not sit still, good luck to you. Re-read this section a few times and be sure to have a good secure hold on the child as the child learns the proper water entries and exits with you. Don't be afraid to ask the lifeguard or one of the other pool members for help. You can ask them to hold your child while you enter the water and then pass the child to you.

How to bring your child into the water if you're already in the pool. Get ready to lift the child into the water.

He's lifting her under her arms in the proper way in the "face-to-face" position.

Toes go over the edge for jumping in because it significantly diminishes the chance that your child will slip.

Entering the water safely by yourself (with a child)

Make sure the child is sitting securely on the deck and you have a hold of him. Put a towel underneath because it is less slippery that way. The child must be able to sit by himself. This child is about ten months old.

Put your arm across the child's body so the child can't fall into the pool. Then do an ease-in entry. See page 42 for more information.

While securing the baby with one hand, you can remove your arm from across the baby's chest and move in front of the child.

Take the child in the face-to-face position, hands under his armpits and "cue" the child (say, "We're going to go into the water now. One, two, three.") Pick him up and bring him into the water with you. Give the child positive feedback: "What a good boy!" or "What a good girl!"

If your child can stand, this is a little more fun for your child.

Stand your child on the edge of the pool. Make sure the child's toes are over the edge, (See page 44 for close-up picture) and you have a firm grip under his armpits. Say, "We're going to go into the water now. Ready. Set. Go!" or "One, two, three," and lift the child.

As you bring the child up and down, say "Weeeee," and bring the child into the water (only to his shoulders—keep head above the water). Keep him in the face-to-face armpit position.

Start walking backwards, drafting (see page 62 for information on drafting.) Remember, the idea is to enjoy your experience.

OTHER USES OF THE STAIRS

Especially if your child is small (but big enough to sit up on his or her own), he or she might enjoy sitting on the steps, and having the feeling of being in the water while feeling something solid underneath him or her. If the pool isn't crowded, it's a good way of introducing the child to the water.

EXITING IN THE DANCE POSITION

Exiting the water is basically the same as entering. Be extra careful because now the baby is wet and your hands are wet. The baby may want to stay because you were having so much fun. The baby might want to wiggle out of your arms or maybe the baby is already wiggling because he or she wants to leave. Either way, take full precautions.

Hold the railing with your free hand. Remember, your hand is wet, so hold the railing tighter.

- Walk up the steps slowly.
- Take one step at a time.
- Cover your child with a towel as soon as possible.
- The evaporating water will make the child feel colder.

This is always safer and easier when there is a significant other or a friend accompanying you. Someone else can hold the child for you when you enter and exit the water.

IF YOUR CHILD CAN SIT OR STAND ON HIS/HER OWN

For a child 18 months or older: There are other ways to do an ease-in entry if your child is older and can sit and/or stand independently.

Unassisted: Sit the child on the edge of the pool while you're in the pool. Put one hand on the child's hand. Always have contact with the child. When you have your child securely by the hand, you do an ease-in entry. When you are in, turn and face the child and then lift the child into the water. Until your child has learned to blow bubbles and put his or her head underwater, keep his or her head above water always.

ROLL OVER AND DROP

Use the following method for children who cannot touch bottom while holding the edge of the pool. Your child should be able to sit and stand on his or her own.

This method is the same as above, except instead of sitting on the edge of the pool and walking on your bottom and lowering yourself in, you roll over on your stomach and wiggle backwards until you drop feet first into the pool. Then you hold the edge of the pool with your hands and lower yourself down until you are in. Both adults and children can use this method. It's especially good if your child is too heavy for you to lift into the pool.

Sit on the edge of the pool.

Start to lean over to your side.

Lay down on your stomach.

Slowly move your body down into the water, but have a firm grip on the side of the pool.

Lower yourself into the water.

I'm in the water. Nice and easy!

Railings are often wet, and children slip. Tell your child to hold the railing firmly. He's already on the top step of the ladder. He's holding both rails and he's ready to go down the ladder, which he cannot see.

He's using his foot to find the first step. Tell your child, "You can't see it. You have to find it with your foot."

Still holding on to the railing, he has found the first step with one foot, then he puts his other foot on the same step.

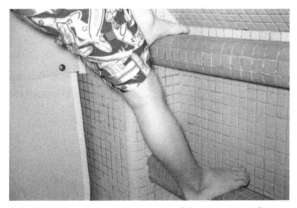

Underwater, you can see him going from the second to the third step.

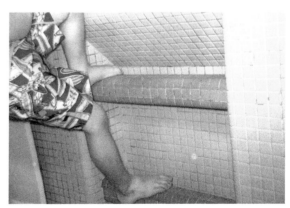

He's found the last step and he's on his way into the pool.

LADDER ENTRY

Why do you have to enter the water backwards? Read the rule on the stairs. It's designed that way to maximize safety. DO NOT DO A LADDER ENTRY WITH AN INFANT. Only do this alone.

This method is the most difficult because you are entering the water "backwards" (facing the wall of the pool), and you can't see the rungs of the ladder. You're also going directly vertically down, so it's much easier to fall backward. You have to find the rungs with your feet. You have to guess where the rungs are until you get familiar with the entry. If you miss a rung, there could be an accident.

The best way to learn to use the ladder is to enter the pool using another method. Climb out using the ladder for the first time. Hold onto the bars with both hands. Make sure you use all the rungs. Try to imagine the distance between the steps when you climb out so you have a feel for the distance when you climb back in. With some pools, there is no top rung and you have to use the side of the gutter or the top of the pool as the top step.

Staircase entrance is always backwards. He holds both rails. It's much easier than a ladder entrance.

The stairs are easier to find with your feet.

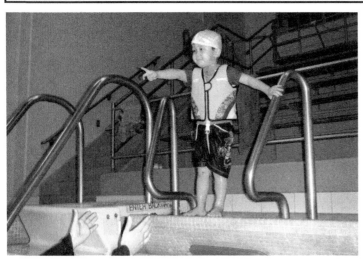

If your child is out of the water and is distracted, and you're in the water, you have to be ready for anything. You may have to get out of the water or move in the water very fast. Note that the parent's hands are ready to receive the child, just in case he jumps. Since he has a PFD on, the parent does not have to worry as much. However, he can still run and fall.

When you get to the bottom you can feel the bottom the pool.

EXITING

The safest and easiest way to exit with an infant or a young child is to ask for help from the lifeguard or another swimmer.

Exiting the water with a small child is simple. Use the dance position, use the stairs and hold the hand rail firmly.

If you're going to exit at a wall without stairs, it's safest to hand the child to another person to hold the baby while you climb out. Always ask the lifeguard for help if there is one. If there isn't another person to help, position a towel near the shallow-end ladder before you get in the pool. When you exit, get as close to the ladder as possible. Put the child on the towel near the edge of the pool with the child's feet toward the pool (so that if the child rolls, he or she rolls away from the pool), and then climb out of the pool yourself.

With an older child, you'll know if the child needs help. Put the child on the ladder ahead of you and let her or him climb out. If the child is well-behaved, tell him or her to walk away from the pool and sit down. If the child is mischievous, tell the child to climb out and hold the railing. Tell your child "Hold the banister. I'm right behind you. Don't move."

With experience getting in and out of the pool, you will find the best way to enter and exit with your child. Always verbally reinforce to your child how important it is only to enter the pool with you. Always remember to have fun. Of course, different places require different skills. You'll have to be creative.

The Hug Position

This is the hug position with cheek on cheek. The child feels very comfortable with your cheeks in contact.

The hug position is very similar to the dance position that was discussed on page 40. This is a position you take in the pool, using the water's buoyancy. With your child facing you, your arms are underneath the child's arms and the child's arms are loosely over your shoulders, like a hug, hence the name.

(The hug position is also called the cheek-to-cheek prone position.)

Try both the dance position and hug position in the water and see which one your child likes best for the times when you are playing in the water.

Until you are ready to teach, you may want to keep your child in the dance position in the water, because once the child is in the hug position, the child is wet up to his or her shoulders. Save the hug position, submersion up to the shoulders, to the end of teaching. Do the dryer stuff at the beginning of your lesson. When you go into the hug position, be attentive to pool time. Once a child gets wet and goes back to the dance position, the child gets colder faster. Watch and make sure your child is staying warm.

An infant should always be in the water less than half an hour. After that, take your child out, dry him or her off, and warm up the child. The hug position also enables you to teach skills that you cannot teach in the dance position. Sometimes when you are teaching, you may find the hug position is better because this position allows the child's legs to be in front of you, so he or she can practice kicking. Also, you can hold your child's legs and show the child the correct way to kick (see Index). With the hug position, you are able to move into other positions easily. The hug position is very similar to the face-to-face armpit position (see Index).

You may find it comfortable to come into the water in the dance position and then put the child in the hug position.

A great thing about the hug position is that you can put your cheek on your child's cheek and make her or him feel very safe. Remember that we are building trust. If the child is not ready to go into other positions, stay in the hug position and walk around backward in the pool. Bend your knees as you move. Go as low as you can and make sure that the child's shoulders are in the water. If you walk backward, you create a nice draft which aids in buoyancy. Be sure to look behind you, so you don't bump into anyone or anything. Moving sideways also works, as does spinning, but moving forward does not provide as much control.

To introduce the idea of kicking:

In the water, hold the child in the hug position. (The child is facing you, with his or her head by or on your shoulder. The child's arms are draped over your shoulders, hugging your neck, and the child can extend his or her legs backward. As you walk backward, your arms move from the hug position to holding your child under his or her armpits. Your hands are supporting your child, cupping his or her ribs. On the side where your child's head is resting, move your arm to support your child's body. Then move your other arm to support the other side. Your arms are under the child's body and your hands move to under the child's legs (anywhere from knee to thigh). Demonstrate the kicking motion with your hands and say, "Kick your feet. Kick your feet. Very good." Your cheek is against your child's cheek. Give the child positive reinforcements: "Magnificent! Superb!" as you are drafting the child backwards and trying to have him or her kick. The child is now in the prone position.

Smaller children kick their whole leg. As they get more confident, allow them to feel their buoyancy more. Still, continue to support them in the water.

Move around the pool in a fun way. Maybe you could sing a song or hum. Make sure the child knows that you are having a good time in the pool. When the child relaxes a little, you are then ready to put the child in a different position.

UNSAFE HOLDS

He's only holding her arm. She can easily slip out of his grip and fall.

When babies don't want to be held, they arch back rapidly, or they collapse into such a relaxed position they slip out of your arms. This is not a safe hold because his right arm is too low on the child's body. His arm should be across her back. One of her legs should be in front of his body and one behind.

SAFER HOLDS

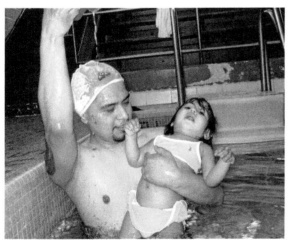

If his arm had been lower, as it was in the previous picture, she would have slipped out of his arms.

This is a correct hold in the dance position. Note that the parent's elbow is high on the child's back and note the position of the child's legs.

Cheek-to-Cheek Position (When the child is on his or her back)

This is the cheek-to-cheek back float position.

The cheek-to-cheek position helps make the child feel safe and comfortable. Therefore, it allows you to teach some skills that your child might be afraid of without that contact. It's what's called a "Swimming Readiness Position." It allows your child to experience the sensation of swimming while being completely supported. This allows the child to relax. It's important that your child learns to be relaxed in the pool. The more relaxed your child is, the more buoyant. It's much easier to swim when you can float.

This position can be used for children of any age from infants up to young children. (It is also good for the child who fears putting his or her head back in the water. Let the child rest his head on your shoulder while you support the child's back. Again, your cheek against the child's cheek gives him confidence that you are right there. You are doing the same thing with your head that he is.

You stand in the water, and your child is suspended in the water by his or her connection to you. Your knees are bent and you are low enough in the water so your shoulders, but not your neck, are nearly underwater. After your child is positioned correctly, on the back, walk backwards so the child can feel the draft.

Say positive things like, "Weeeee" and "This is fun!" If the child likes it, great. If the child doesn't like it, stop. Come back at another time when the child has practiced and is comfortable with previous skills.

Use extra caution here. Assure your child you won't get the child's face wet. Do not let water splash the face (it runs down the nostrils and scares the child. Water in the ears is ok). The child will only float if his ears are in the water. Introduce this idea slowly. One ear at a time. Don't juggle your child or get the head wet. When your child is on his or her back, your child can't hang on to you. From this position, your child can't see you. You must be very supportive.

(If your child is not yet comfortable putting his or her ears in the water, go back to the Index and find where we discuss getting ears wet.) If there's another participating person, have that person move along with you and say, "Kick your feet. Very good." The other person can also gently hold and move your child's legs to show how the kicking motion feels. Let go when your child starts to move his legs on his own. Praise him for this.

This skill helps the child begin to learn the Elementary Backstroke, and it also helps the child learn how to kick on his or her back. Remember to always walk backward and use the drafting technique when using the cheek-to-cheek position.

Also remember: when you're teaching this skill, have fun and enjoy it. Also, always let the child learn at his or her own pace. That's what the parents have to learn.

The Face-to-Face Position

The face-to-face position is important for infants and toddlers because it allows you to see your child's face and the child to see yours. The face-to-face position makes your child more comfortable. Funny faces will make your child happier. You can smile to reassure your child. You can see your child's expression, and if the child is uncomfortable, move him or her closer to you. The closer a child is to you, the safer a child feels.

To put your child in the face-to-face position, hold the child or infant underneath the armpits and have the child directly in front of you. This position is good for practicing skills such as your walking backwards and drafting the child while your child kicks her or his feet. It's also a good position if the child is a little more advanced. You can lower the child down a little bit in the water (so the chin is near the water) while the child kicks his or her feet. You can ask your child to blow bubbles. This is also a good position for blowing bubbles without kicking feet.

When kids can kick and blow bubbles together, they are ready for the side-to-side position.

Face-to-face armpit position

Parent beginning to draft— the parent is starting to walk backwards, the child is drafting. Good hand position. The parent is really enjoying the experience of teaching her son aquatics.

The child's face is closer to the water.

Bubble-blowing

Blowing bubbles is the first step to correct use of breath in the water. This is a crucial skill your child will use in all swimming experiences. Learning how to blow bubbles helps to develop breath control and endurance.

Bubble-blowing is a skill that may be do-able for your child at 18 months or older. We've seen it much earlier and much later. Children can usually blow bubbles by the age of 24 months. They can start earlier if parents practice with them at home. See below for more ideas about this.

Into the Bathtub

The bathtub, during bath time at home, is a good place to introduce bubble blowing. All these exercises should be introduced **before** you get soap in the water because soap can sting your child's eyes. Swimming readiness skills must be taught in safety.

You can get a **ping-pong ball** so your child can practice blowing it across the surface of the tub or the pool. This is an excellent way to learn breath control. Anything kids can do that's fun—so they don't even realize they're learning—is good. As your child gets better at blowing on a ping-pong ball, let his lips get closer to the water.

Not only is the child blowing the ping-pong ball, he's also moving his arms and legs under the water unconsciously trying to catch up with the ball.

The ball is moving away, and he's getting another deep breath so he can blow the ball again. All the time he's getting positive feedback from his grandfather, "Great job! You blew the ball far!" The grandfather could bring in a second ping-pong ball and say, "Let's have a race now." (Always let the child win.)

He blew the ball away again, and now he's moving his arms and legs. Mike likes to invite the child to take the ball home and draw on it, saying, "We'll bring it back with us next time."

Making Ripples. Cup your hands together, hold water in them, and put your bottom lip on the water and blow ripples. This can also be done at the pool. Then have your child try to blow ripples across the water. An infant or toddler is not old enough to make the cup with her hands: this is something you have to do for her. Your child can also put her bottom lip to the water in the tub or pool and blow ripples.

Place your bottom lip as close to the water as you can, or even in the water, and then blow the water, just like you would blow the ping-pong ball.

Humming. For this exercise, you may have to join your child in the tub. At first, when you demonstrate in the water, put just your mouth in the water and make a humming noise as you do it. Keep your mouth closed. Ask your child to try. Keep the child's nose out of the water. Often children are frightened when their noses go in. The idea is to have a good time when you are learning humming.

Blowing bubbles. Your child may be game to blow bubbles but not to hum. Try this next: Blow bubbles with just your mouth in the water. Show your child and ask your child to try it too. Ask you child who can "make the loudest motorboat." Start making noise before you put your mouth in the water. The motorboat noise is "BRRRRR." Blow bubbles and make noise while you're blowing. Ask your child to try that too. If your child is quiet, you can say, "What, you got a muffler on that?" or "You're in a sailboat?'

Perhaps make outrageous claims, such as, "I am the noisiest motorboat in the world." Then say, "I take a deep breath of air and then I let the air out in the water. Just my mouth is in the water." Then demonstrate.

Straw? Use the following method at your own discretion. Avoid telling a child to do something wrong or that will later make you yell, "Stop! Don't do that! It's annoying!" If you believe that teaching a child to blow bubbles through a straw could lead to your yelling, use another method. The method is as follows: If your child wants to figure out how to blow bubbles, you can take a straw and have her or him make bubbles in a drink. Children love to do this. You might create a monster who likes to do this too much, but for the sake of our purpose of a greater good, allow the child to blow bubbles in the glass. Once you tell your child how well he or she is doing, then show the child how to blow air through the straw to make the pinwheel spin. You could also show your child how to use a straw to blow bubbles in the tub.

He's learning from his big sister.
(see photo below)

Some children can't get the concept of blowing bubbles. The straw gives them a great tool to show them exactly what to do. Once you take the straw away, they know exactly how to blow bubbles: they do the same thing without the straw.

Children's Concerns

Children often are concerned that water will go in their mouths. Remind your child, "Water can't go in your mouth when you're blowing bubbles." If your child is blowing bubbles that means he or she is not swallowing water. This is a good skill for a young person to have when learning about swimming pools.

In a pool, your mouth's going to go in the water, and if you get a mouthful of water you may panic. So, teach your child to blow bubbles whenever he or she puts his or her face in the water. If you have your child do that, the child will learn to do it automatically. It lets the child learn faster because he or she won't get sidetracked by a mouthful of water.

Learning Breath Control/ Blowing Bubbles

Here are skills that you can teach your child either before going to the pool or in the pool. These are called "Swimming Readiness Skills." Often at around a year old, a child is ready to learn these skills. If you try these things and they aren't fun for your child, wait a few weeks and try again.

No need to push. There's plenty of time. All children learn at different rates. If the child already has fear, it will take a little longer because you must remove the fear first and then begin teaching the skill. This takes time.

Fear is real. Do not push your child. If you push, you may push your child backward. Praise your child. For example, use words like, "Outstanding! Excellent!" **Teach when you have had enough sleep. Be aware of your own attitude.** Your child will pick up on it. You want this to be pleasurable for both of you.

Start Out of the Water: Blow Air

Model this for your child. Make a circle with your lips like you're going to whistle, but not quite so tight. Blow out air. You want to feel the force of air coming out. Put your hand up to your mouth to feel it. Have your child put his or her hand up to feel the force of his or her own blowing.

Explanation for adults only: When you blow bubbles with your mouth small, like when you whistle, the air takes longer to escape from your mouth. This builds pressure in your head. Because the air pressure in your head is greater than the pressure outside, this helps keep water from going up your nose and in your mouth. It won't prevent it, but it helps. We're trying to teach that whenever the child puts the head in the water, he or she should blow bubbles. This way the child won't get a mouth full of water and won't get afraid of putting his or her face in the water. Your child has to learn this to become a swimmer.

A key to teaching is that children love to try things parents do. The child will mimic you. So demonstrate, and make it fun.

Buy a pinwheel from a local toy store and teach your child how to blow on it to make it spin. This is helpful to learn breath control for swimming. You blow the pinwheel first to show the child how it works. Puff your cheeks up and enjoy making that blowing noise. Then let your child try. This is a skill you can begin at home.

Never say, "You're doing it wrong."

Say instead, "Let me show you," or "There's a better way," or "You can improve that." Give only one correction at a time.

A Small Bottle of Bubbles

If your child has the habit of sticking out their tongue and putting it in the water, demonstrate blowing bubbles with a small bottle of bubbles. Blow bubbles and see if your child will mimic you. Then try blowing bubbles at home or at the pool with a straw, or blowing bubbles with your child in the pool.

From a toy store, buy a bottle of blowing bubbles. Children love to see the bubbles go. Demonstrate and then let your child try it. If your child sticks his or her tongue out and tries to lick the water, your child is not ready to blow bubbles.

When the child can blow soap bubbles, it's time to lower both his lips into the water and say, "Blow bubbles!"

At home you can have the child practice. Give the child a bottle of bubbles and say, "Practice blowing your bubbles." Notice the life vest. He's at home and he's practicing for the pool by wearing his vest.

Review blowing bubbles at home. Say to your child, "Do you remember how to blow bubbles? Let's try again. Let's see." After your child demonstrates, you blow bubbles and make noise. "Can you make noise while you do it?" Listen to your child. Ask the child to make more noise if you can't hear it, "I can't hear you." "I still can't hear you." Words of praise: "Sensational." "Tremendous."

What we're working toward, much later, is putting it all together: the bubble blowing, paddling and the kicking.

If your child fears putting her face in the water, try putting your hands together to form a cup, and putting your face in your cupped hands to blow bubbles.

If your child is afraid of putting his face in the water, draft your child, and put your face in the water and blow bubbles. While you are holding your child, ask your child to mimic you.

This is an older child who has a lot of fear, but she's holding on to the edge of the pool, and was told to hold her breath and put her face in the water and count to three. Then, her job was to pick her face up out of the water.

If a child does not want to put his or her face in the water, Mike likes to sing, "Pop goes the weasel!" He tells them ahead of time, that when he says, "Pop!" everyone puts their face in the water including him. If they don't do it the first time, he says, "Uh-oh. We'll try it again. I don't think one of the weasels put their face in the water!" This often works.

One, two, three, and out of the water!

The next step is to ask the child to put his or her whole head underwater and blow bubbles. Notice this is an older child. Younger children cannot do this unless you hold their hands.

When your child is ready to learn, your child will learn.

If in any one session, your child's head goes underwater three times, end the session. Words of praise: good job!

Drafting

What is drafting? If you put a ping-pong ball in the water and then place your hand in next to it, as you move your hand away from the ball, it will follow your hand. Think of the ping-pong ball as the person being taught and the hand as the teacher.

Drafting is a technique used to teach someone to swim. This technique helps the learner move more easily in the water. This helps give her or him confidence during the learning process.

Most of the time when you are drafting, you are walking backwards, supporting your child with your hands. When you walk backwards, the water around you will move with you and the water around the child will also move with you. This helps make learning swimming skills easier for the child.

This technique is used in coordination with most of the elementary skills. It's good for learning to float and learning the Elementary Backstroke. The child will gain a little more confidence when he or she experiences drafting because the movement creates lift in the water. That will make the child feel more relaxed which will also give her or him more buoyancy and make the skill easier to learn.

Depending on the age of your child and your child's ability to blow bubbles or kick feet, as you're drafting you can say, "Blow bubbles," or "Kick your feet." Always give the child positive feedback, "Wonderful job" "You're the greatest."

If you are already drafting, you can also try to put your child in the Hug Position, cheek-to-cheek, reach your arms underneath the child until you get to his or her legs, and move them up and down, simulating kicking. Say, "Kick your feet. Kick your feet." Then say, "Fantastic! You really kick your feet well." Reward anything with praise.

You can also start with the child on his back. Most drafting occurs when you're holding the top of the child's head against your chest, and put your hands underneath the child's back for support. Now start to walk backwards. This is good if a child is rigid and fearful. "Relax. Move your arms. I won't let your face get wet. Don't worry."

For a little less drafting and more independence, put one hand under the child's chin and the other hand under the back of his head as you walk backwards. Hold the child's face out of the water at all times.

For the least amount of drafting, do not hold the child at all. While the child is doing the skill, just walk behind, staying close. Your body will help pull your child along. Sometimes the child realizes he is floating and grabs your hand. When the child realizes he is floating solo, he is ready for Elementary Backstroke.

In the pool: the side-to-side/prone position

The side-to-side position is for children with some comfort in the water. You walk next to your child while holding the child. It's a more advanced skill. If your child clings to you or the child is rigid in water then he or she is not ready. Work on other skills and come back to it later.

The side-to-side position is a little more advanced but can be used for infants and toddlers. The side-to-side position is also known as the prone position.

You have to be careful with the transition into this position because you don't want to lose control of your child. That could cause the child's head to go underwater—a setback—and could create fear. The goal is to have the child tummy-down in the water with his or her head always up above the water. Your support helps the child keep his or her head up. Words of praise: Outstanding! Excellent.

This is an older child. The parent is holding the child in the side-to-side position for the long Doggy Paddle. The child keeps her head out of the water. The parent stands still. To be able to do the long Doggy Paddle, children need to be able to do three things: kick their feet, blow bubbles and paddle their arms.

Put the child up against your body and support the child. The child is horizontal in the water: make sure that you keep the child's head out of the water. You can lower the child a little so the child can feel his or her buoyancy in the water.

Do this carefully. You do not want to drop your child. Holding your child steady on your body in the transition gives your child security and confidence.

The parent is starting to walk forward in the side-to-side position. She tells the child, "Paddle your arms and kick your feet."

Now the parent adds blowing bubbles to the sequence, and says, "Blow bubbles now." The child is paddling, blowing bubbles and kicking. You can correct weaknesses in the stroke by saying, "Reach out further and pull down." "Put your whole face in the water and blow bubbles." "Don't kick so hard."

The side-to-side position allows the parent to support the child while teaching three skills. This is a very safe position to teach in because you can have a secure hold on your child. You also can gradually release your hold and let the child feel buoyant in the water. If your child sinks, you can immediately re-establish your hold, creating the feeling of safety. Your hands are still on the child while the child learns to swim independently. Tell the child to use all three skills, "Paddle your arms, kick, and blow bubbles."

How to turn your child from the face-to-face position to the back armpit position —holding your child so she's facing away from you.

These two positions allow you to do so much. In the face-to-face position you can walk backwards, draft your child, and say, "Kick your feet and blow bubbles." You can also go to the hug position, cheek-to-cheek. From the back position, you can put your child's head on your shoulder and walk backwards and start to teach your child to kick his or her feet while the child is on his or her back. Or you can start to teach the child to put her ears in the water, float, or do the easy Elementary Backstroke. These two positions which you, the adult, are learning, are the start of teaching all the skills for the beginning swimmer.

This is where you start when you want to turn your child around. This is the face-to-face armpit position.

These instructions are for the right-handed parent. If you are left-handed, switch all rights to lefts. With each step you take, talk with your child and tell the child what you are doing. Always offer encouragement.

From the face-to-face position, holding the child under the armpits, turn the child's torso counterclockwise so their right side will touch your chest. Say, "Good job."

Hold the child there with your right hand. Switch hands—remove the right hand from the left side of your child, under the armpit of the child. Replace your right hand with your left hand. Say, "You're doing great."

Keep constant light pressure to support your child against your body. Now your right hand is free.

Put your right hand under the right side of the child, under her armpit. Make sure you hold your child tightly against your chest with your right arm. You want to be extra careful so your child doesn't slip. The younger your child, the easier for the child to slip. Say, "We're doing this perfectly." It's OK to include yourself.

When you have your right hand under the right armpit, slide your left hand under the left armpit. You can say, "Wow, this is good."

Make sure you have a good grip on your child. Now you have your child in the back armpit position. You can put your child to the side (either right or left depending on where you are most comfortable). Then you can start to walk forward and lower your child's chest into the water.

Now that you have the child in a new hold, you can put the child in the prone or side-to-side position, where you are walking in the water next to your child while holding her. Talk with your child as you do this and tell her what's going on.

After you have your child in the side-to-side position, you can lower the child's chest into the water and say, "Paddle your arms and kick your feet," as you walk forward holding her. You can do this with most children eighteen months old and older. If your child can blow bubbles, you can ask her to blow bubbles while you do this. It's very difficult for children to do three things at once. Please start with teaching the child to move the arms, or kick. Later, add blowing bubbles.

This can also be used in reverse to move your child back to the cheek-to-cheek position. The side-to-side position is great for teaching the three basic swimming skills: blowing bubbles, paddling your arms, and kicking your feet. In the pool, you can walk, holding the child, and say, "Kick your feet." Always give the child positive feedback ("terrific" "great"), then tell the child to "paddle your arms." If the child is able to do that, try adding bubble-blowing to the mix. With practice, you can allow the buoyancy of the water to hold your child while he or she is swimming. You do this by releasing your hold very gradually.

Another helpful hint: if you are in the water with another person, or near a wall, you can have the child swim toward the person or the wall. You say to your child, "You can do it! Pull hard!" Make sure you know the child has the buoyancy to swim those few strokes on his or her own. This is a great confidence builder. Tell the child how great he or she has done. Tell the child he or she is a champion. Whether infant, child or adult, the person will then want to try again.

Learning anything—to play the violin, to speak another language, to swim—takes practice and effort. Practice often. Take time. And give your child your attention. The rewards are priceless.

Paddling Arms

Paddling arms is a "swimming readiness skill" which means you are getting your child ready to swim and the child is getting a sense of the basic movements. If your child is small, a safe way to paddle arms is as follows. You, the adult, put your back against the wall of a swimming pool. Lift one leg, sit the child on your leg, and raise the leg high enough so that the child's shoulders are out of the water. Then take both of the child's hands and put them in the palms of your hands, as flat as possible.

Then extend one arm at a time and say, "Paddle your arms." As you do this, say, "Look! You're paddling your arms." This is how the child learns. Later when you're doing a face-to-face position movement with your child, and you say, "Paddle your arms," the child will know what to do. This is discussed in more detail later in the book when we talk about swimming skills.

This parent is practicing paddling arms with his daughter. Do not do this more than a few minutes. If the child is enjoying it you can keep going, but try to stop before they stop enjoying it.

A Few Early Words to Parents

Your expectations are pressure on your child that may get in the way of the fun *and the learning* of being in the water. Expect to enjoy yourself and to help your child have fun. Try to go in prepared to teach, prepared to have fun, but without expectations about what your child can accomplish that day. Your child learns in her or his own time. Take satisfaction in trying to do something for your kids, and be patient with yourself as you figure out the best way to

Notice how the parent is enjoying
the time with her baby.

do this so your child is safe, and you have a good time together.

Make sure you, the adult, have all your equipment in place. You are organized. You have a plan. You are well-prepared. Be polite. Choose a quiet area so distractions are limited.

Be sensitive to your child's limits and fears. Prepare mentally and physically. Listen carefully. If a child says, "Do I have to do that?", consider trying another skill. We have decades of experience with swimming. We know name-calling does not work. Never say anything derogatory about gender or race. Never insult or threaten your child. Never say, "You're doing it all wrong." If you insult your child, that is baggage the kid will carry for the rest of his or her life.

Encouragement does work. Do praise your child. We include suggested words of praise throughout this book. Try, "That's right." "Good." "You're getting better every time!" or "Great job." Or "Let's see if we can make it easier for you… Let me show you a little secret." "There you go."

It's an art to be able to be kind and tell your child the truth. Practice that art. Telling the truth breeds trust. That helps with the learning process. As Mike says, "I believe in honesty but not in sheer stupidity." Tell the truth in a productive way or you will get in the way of your child's learning. Your child is going to do things that look awkward to you. Be kind.

If you're teaching a skill that is hard or your child is getting bored, switch to teaching another skill or sing a song or play a game, and do not go back to teaching the same skill that day. For example, if you're teaching something in the prone position, teach something in another position.

Do go in the water with your kids. You have to teach gradually. If you go in trying to teach a too-advanced skill, it won't work, and it won't be fun. Start with basic skills. Reassure your children. Review each skill until the child is comfortable and confident. Give clear directions, but don't give too many. Give feedback for one problem at a time. Correct the biggest problem first.

Don't make your child do anything he or she doesn't want to do. Children learn well if they're not afraid. In the early phases of learning, your child's gaining confidence and having fun in the water is far more important than learning how to swim a specific stroke.

We like to give the child options because a lot of things we try don't work for individual children. So we try it another way. And if that fails, we try a third way. And if that fails, maybe the child isn't ready for that skill. Then we go back a step or two. We believe in teaching this way because we've found this method works.

Eventually, your child will see others doing it and he or she will want to try, too. There is one exception. If a child's been in the water before, sometimes the child doesn't want to get in again because it's a little cold or it's a change, or the child could be very fussy, or the child needs a nap. If you wait for a child to come in the pool, you may wait your whole life. You can't really rush fun, but your time is limited. The ones who can do it on their own we don't push in. With an infant or a toddler who won't come in, we advise you wait one or two times, and then simply pick the child up and enter the water (see the Index for the correct position). Children who cry take lessons, but once the child gets in the water, and the child knows the parent is alright and the and the other children are alright, the child starts to calm down and have fun. All you want to do for the next lesson or two is walk around and enjoy the water with the child. Then by the following lesson the child is usually ready to start learning. Each time you're in the water with your child, make sure the last thing you do in the water is something fun, so the child wants to come back.

Of course we would never recommend bribery, but we've seen this work at the doctor's office, and it can work poolside for young children. Sometimes at the end of swimming, you can offer a lollipop, a seashell or a toy the child can enjoy and play with only at the pool. That makes swimming a pleasant memory. For instance, you can say next time, "Mr. Ducky is at the pool. Do you want to see him?" Mr. Ducky splashes your child. Let your child splash Mr. Ducky, or even use a favorite sponge from the kitchen and be creative to remind your child of the fun at the pool.

Again, keep your child in the water less than half an hour. Otherwise, the child will get cold and remember that feeling. He or she may not want to return.

If your child is tall enough to stand in the shallow end of the pool.

When children are big enough to stand in the water, they don't need a parent to hold them all the time, but they do need someone to watch, coach and help them.

What do you do with a child who can't stand in the shallow end but wants to learn to swim?

If your child is too old for infant pre-school aquatics, then flotation devices can help. You can go into the water with floaties (see section on flotation devices in the Index), and start teaching him or her how to swim. You must always be in the water with the child.

Words of praise: "That's the way to do it! Way to go!"

Fears about positions

Bigger kids are often more scared of learning to swim than younger kids, who don't yet know to be afraid. We teach the elementary positions first, and let the child get acclimated to the water. We try to remove the fear and build trust, to make the child feel secure and safe, and have fun. Then we move on to the next more advanced position. If you go to the next position and see fear on your child's face (we explain fear signs in each section), go back to the less advanced position and just have fun. Try again later.

If you get frustrated, you might not be the right person to teach your child swimming skills. Some parents get disappointed that their child is not accomplishing things at the rate the parent thinks is the right speed. They take it personally, as if the child is an extension of them, and not as if the child is a unique, separate person. If you are that sort of parent, and you want your child to learn to swim, enroll the child in a swim class, and do not sit on the bleachers during class with that terrible expression on your face.

Sometimes as hard as a parent tries, the child has difficulty learning from the parent. As children get older, especially sometimes as they turn eight or nine years old, they may become difficult for reasons we don't know. You might be better off hiring a professional, or giving this book to someone the child trusts and let that person give it a try.

Introducing water to the face: For adults or young people
Walking to the deep end

Here are some of the skills adults need to make them better teachers.

People take it for granted that all adults can swim. Our experience is so many adults cannot swim and have such a fear of swimming that they won't go near the water. Some even lie about it.

Once we are in the pool, we want to get our faces wet. This can be a very difficult skill for people who fear putting their face in the water. They fear drowning. Take this seriously. Allow the person to take his or her time to get used to putting his or her face in the water. It's often good to watch other people in a public swim area and see that others are OK when they put their faces in the water.

After the adult or young person gets his or her face wet, even if the person is not adjusted to the water, a good way to have her or him adjust is to walk back and forth in the pool, each time getting lower in the water. With one hand, the person can hold the side of the pool so he or she feels secure. The person can walk to the deep end up to the shoulders, turn around, hold the side of the pool with the other hand and walk back. Repeat this as many times as necessary until the person starts to feel relaxed. When the person gets relaxed, have the person walk to shoulder-level water and face the wall. Hold the wall with both hands. Now have the person submerge his or her face in the water for three seconds maximum. If the person is blowing bubbles in the low end, you can have the person try to blow bubbles in the deep end.

As a parent, this is something you must be able to do before you can teach it. As you practice this, you desensitize yourself to the fear of it, and this helps to desensitize your child.

You do the same procedure when teaching your child. As the child gets more confident, when the child holds the wall, the child can pretend to be playing the piano with the fingers. This way the child doesn't lose the grip, but the child is not really holding on.

Introducing water to the face, different methods

Your child's face gets wet when in the pool. Your child must be prepared, understand and realize what will happen if his or her face gets wet.

Stand in the shallow end of the pool facing each other and hold hands. As the experienced person, you demonstrate this skill to your partner.

Close your eyes, hold your breath, and put your face in the water for less than two seconds. Then ask your child to try it. "You wash your face in the morning. It's no big deal." You just want the child to get the feel of water on the face.

For some adults this is so scary, the person acts like a movie vampire putting the face in holy water. You can demonstrate this with other people or have the person put water in cupped hands and put his face in it to show it doesn't hurt. If the person can't do it the first time, just coninue with the rest of the lessons and try again next time. Even if a person comes out of the water afraid, praise the person. It can change fear to joy.

Words of praise: "Outstanding. Super! I'm amazed!"

Blowing Bubbles, for Children and Adults

Practicing blowing bubbles at home is helpful before you introduce this skill in the pool. Kids have no fear of blowing bubbles. What they often lack is the skill to blow bubbles. That's why you should try to teach this before the child gets in the pool. The child can also learn this skill in the pool. What builds fear is progressing too fast. Your child will fear swallowing water if he or she can't blow bubbles. Take your time, go slowly. Make sure your child is comfortable blowing bubbles. You want to build confidence.

Also, for adults: this skill is very important because whenever one's face is in the water, one is going to be blowing bubbles (exhaling).

Tell your child that when you blow bubbles, you want to make your mouth small, like you are whistling.

Face your child in the water. Start by making a cup with your two hands, pick up pool water, put your chin in the water and blow ripples. Then have your child try. Then submerge your face to your nostrils and blow bubbles or hum. Then submerge your whole face and blow bubbles. Then tell your child it's his or her turn to repeat what you just did. Repeat these skills until everyone is comfortable.

Words of praise: "I could not have done it better myself. Awesome!"

See page 56 for more data on ping-pong balls and breathing.

Sisters underwater. Notice that the younger sister has her eyes open and the older sister has her eyes shut. Because the younger child wasn't told to be afraid of opening her eyes, she wasn't.

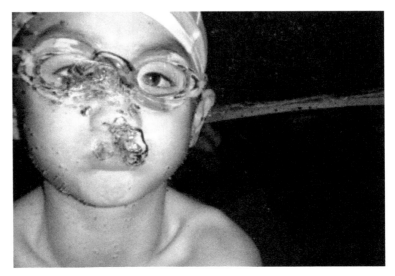

Goggles help. They allow children to open their eyes underwater. When you do put your face in the water, goggles can prevent your eyes from being affected by chlorine, and they help you see better.

Putting Whole Head Underwater (submerging)

The next section of this book is about blowing bubbles and opening eyes underwater. It's important to get your whole head underwater and blow bubbles. There are a lot of different skills and techniques that we can use to teach this.

First teach yourself, then teach your child. **If you are not an experienced swimmer,** this is a step-by-step guide. **If you are an experienced swimmer,** you need to practice breaking down the parts of the lesson into small manageable child-sized bites. It's often hard for skilled people to make things simple enough so children can learn.

If your child has problems with one skill, sometimes it is easier to move on to the next one so the child does not get frustrated. Sometimes children learn something a strange way before they learn the right way, and that's OK as long as they're safe. They may come up with their own version before they can do it the "proper way."

Blink instead of rubbing your eyes. BLINKING YOUR EYES IS A CRUCIAL BEGINNER'S SKILL

If your child can blow bubbles in the water, demonstrate submerging your face while in the water and blowing bubbles, then come up, take a breath and repeat. Once your child is ready to be introduced to a new skill (after the child has mastered the old one), try showing the child the next level. Say, "Can you put your whole face in and blow bubbles?" Show your child. When you bring your head up, blink to get the water out of your eyes. Don't rub your eyes. Say, "Don't forget to blink when you come up."

FOR ADULTS ONLY: When you have mastered these skills, breathe in and put your head under the water again. This time, however, do not go so fast. Try to stay submerged until you have exhaled all your air. When you have finished exhaling, straighten your knees and bring your head out of the water. Stand to inhale. Practice this at least ten times, until you start to become relaxed with it.

Words of praise: "Terrific."

The Importance of Blinking
You should know this before you go to the deep end.

The reason for blinking your eyes and not rubbing is that when your child's or your arms are in the water, they help hold you up. Your arms are very buoyant. When you start to move in to the deeper end of the pool, you need your arms in the water for buoyancy. In the deep end, you do not want to have to lift your arms out of the water to rub the water out of your eyes. If you lift your arms out of the water, it will give you less buoyancy, which may cause your head to lower under the water again. Having your head go back under the water because you are rubbing your eyes may cause you to panic (and drink water) because you are not ready for that.

Knowing how to blink your eyes to remove the water will help you in future swimming endeavors.

One way to learn to blink is to stand in the shallow end and to hold hands with the partner or person you are teaching. After the person submerges and comes up for air say, "Don't rub your eyes. Just blink!" It's a normal reaction to try to rub the water out of your eyes. If you hold the person's hands, he or she can't rub the eyes and has to try blinking. The person will have better success with the skill. Not-rubbing-your-eyes takes some practice to get used to. If the child says, "It's stinging my eyes," tell the child, "You only have to do it once," and the child should try to wear swimming goggles from now on. This is also true for adults. However, do not let adults wear goggles until the adult tries this skill. This skill is very important for later advancement, especially in treading water, changing positions, and water entries and exits.

Opening the eyes underwater can be the most challenging experience for a beginner. Opening the eyes underwater can sting. Vision is blurry. It's a different experience. But like other skills, this is an important one.

Words of praise: "Good job! Wonderful!"

Flutter Kicking

The first kick you teach your child is the flutter kick. You do the same kick on your back as you do on your stomach.

Have the child sit at the edge of the wall, and then slide forward as close to the edge as he or she can (without the rear end falling in the pool) and lean back on his or her hands. Tell the child to let his or her weight go on the arms and to not let the legs touch the water, and "Point those toes!" The parent should be standing in front of the child, but be in the water. Then tell the child to kick the feet out of the water while pointing toes. Tell the child, "Don't touch the water." Give positive feedback: "Great job!"

It is OK if the child's knees bend a little. Tell the child to lean back on the arms and continue kicking feet. You can hold the child's toes and move them up and down to show the child how to kick.

For the flutter kick, feet should kick from six inches to twelve inches apart at the widest part of the kick. When the big toes pass each other, they should not touch, but should be next to one another. As the child gets more skilled with kicking, you can tell the child that, "Whether you are on your stomach or on your back in the pool, you always kick hard down toward the bottom of the pool, and easy up toward the sky."

Be sure to tell the child again to point toes! An important part of learning this skill is to have the child close his or her eyes and think how the kicking feels. Tell the child to try to remember that feeling. "Do you feel how that feels? Remember that, because that is how the kick should feel when you're in the water."

This is a teenaged girl on a swimming team demonstrating the perfect kick.

Do this skill for a few minutes. This skill will be very tiring for your child. Do not continue to teach this for too long.

Now have your child get in the pool, and go to the side of the pool. Your child can face you and hold your hands. Support the child while she tries to kick her feet. Watch the child's feet and ask her to try to get the same feeling that she had on the deck. (Don't expect the child to kick very well now. Much later on, when the child does start to put her head in the water, and the child's feet start to rise in the water, she will again feel what she felt on deck and know this is proper kicking.) Don't allow the child's feet to come completely out of the water. You don't want the child to kick the air. Say, "Keep your feet in the water." Don't do this a long time because it's very tiring for your child. Tell the child, "Listen for splashing." Be sure to have your child look straight ahead at you. Don't let the child turn her head because that will make her feet sink. Say, "Great job. You're kicking really well!"

More Kicking Skills Practice

If you're in a larger pool with a gutter or edge your child can hold on to, you can stand next to your child or walk behind her and help her get started by holding her feet and moving them up and down in the proper position. Then you can let them go and say, "Try it on your own." Any effort should be complimented: "Good kicking skills." This should be practiced in thirty-second intervals each time you go to the pool. Gradually work up to one minute. Only do it longer if your child enjoys it and does not seem to be tiring.

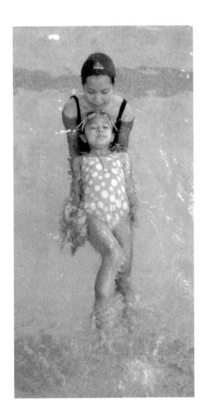

Walking backward, the parent holds the child while teaching kicking. It causes drafting, which helps the child stay afloat.

Kicking and Blowing Bubbles at the Same Time
A more advanced skill

Review the section on blowing bubbles (see Index).

This is what a younger child looks like as he's learning to kick and blow bubbles.

Have the child get in the water and hold the side of the pool. If the pool doesn't have a gutter on the side which is easy to hold, you may use a kick board. The best way to do that is for you to hold one end of the board while your child holds the other end. If you don't have a kick board, you can hold the child's hands in your hands near the surface of the water. Tell the child to kick while keeping his head out of the water. Tell the child to make "baby splashes" while kicking. Remind your child, "Listen to your feet. Don't look at your feet," because if your child turns his head to look at his feet, the feet will drop well below the water line. Keep reminding your child to look straight ahead and listen to the kicking.

The lower your face is in the water, the easier it is to kick. This is our teenaged swimming team member. With a younger child, do not expect this much.

This is a child using the kick board, blowing bubbles, and using his feet. Blow the bubbles out slowly, and then…

He picks his head up and takes a quick breath. Then he repeats the pattern. If your child fears swallowing water, make sure he breathes in completely before he puts his head back in the water. The child can start to blow out as he's putting his head back in. That way he won't take in any water.

When the child is comfortable doing this, ask your child if he can blow bubbles while kicking. Tell the child to make the mouth small and blow bubbles. When he finishes this, ask if it is easier blowing bubbles and kicking or if it is easier to keep your head out of the water and kick. The child will probably find that blowing bubbles and kicking is easier. The right answer is, "Blowing bubbles and kicking," because if the head is in the water, kicking is much easier. But your child may have a different answer and that's OK.

This is a difficult skill. Do not let your child do this for a long time. Move on to something more fun.

Teaching one skill at a time

Introduce one skill at a time: blowing bubbles, paddling your arms, kicking your feet. When the child has dexterity with the first skill, teach the second. By the time the child can do all three, he or she is ready to start learning to swim. If your child can do these three things together, the child is still NOT SAFE. The child needs a PFD and your supervision is mandatory.

This is the jellyfish float. Try this before you teach it. Stand in the low end of the pool about chest deep. Take a deep breath and hold it. Put your face in the water. Totally relax, and let your legs lift off the bottom and float up. The back of your head should be out of the water. Most times you have to hold a person's hands as they learn this. Hold the child's hands to help him feel secure.

If you want to learn to float and you don't have anyone to help you, you can start by holding the edge of the pool or the ladder, and try floating while holding on with one hand. As you get more relaxed, try "playing the piano" with your hand, meaning, relax your grip and move your fingers up and down the bar.

Floating and Buoyancy

This skill requires your practice beforehand. Go through all the steps in the water before showing your child so you know what it feels like. You can tell someone about something until you are blue in the face, but if you experience it beforehand, that can help make you a superior teacher.

Some people float easily. Others do not. In part, this is because there are two kinds of people: "positive buoyant" and "negative buoyant." A negative buoyant person is someone who needs to use movement to stay on the water's surface. A positive buoyant person has to use movement and work to stay *under* the surface of the water. If you are positive buoyant you float much more easily than someone who is negative buoyant. If you have no fear of the water, and sink while you are trying to float, you are negative buoyant. You can still learn to float after you learn some basic movements that will help you float. See the Index for the Elementary Backstroke.

Jellyfish Float

You can't teach the jellyfish float until the person is comfortable putting his face in the water. He doesn't have to be able to blow bubbles: he can hold his breath and close his eyes.

The jellyfish float and the back float are taught one right after the other.

When teaching this skill, what the parent looks for first is buoyancy or lack of buoyancy. You do this by doing the Jellyfish Float.

But first, tell your child how to recover.

Recovery from the Jellyfish Float. Your hands have to be open and flat.

How to recover: From the prone position, your child puts her hands in front of her head in the water like Superman, and pushes her hands down toward the bottom of the pool. At the same time, your child bends her knees towards her chest. This lifts her head out of the pool. While this motion is happening, the child steadies her feet and stands. Sometimes your child may have to repeat the arm motion twice to achieve this. Say, "It's like jumping rope forward." Demonstrate.

For people who are very nervous or for someone who is doing this for the first time, teach this in phases. First, hold the bottom of the child's hands. Tell the child to take a deep breath and hold it, and put her face in the water, and then let the child float. Don't use a lot of pressure to support the child, just enough so she knows there's someone there. A lot of people won't start floating, so the parent can take a few steps backward while holding the child's hands. This causes the child's legs to come off the bottom and start floating. Praise your child. "Marvelous!"

What you are looking for is that the back of the child's head is out of the water. This means that when the child is on her back, the child's face will be out of the water. This means she is buoyant.

Next time, before the child is holding your hands, tell your child, "You're going to try playing the piano on my hands." This allows your child to loosen the grip on you and move the fingers up and down. The child also does this while holding her breath (up to about ten or twenty seconds). Then, continue with the lesson at the top of the page. Word of praise: Super!

If you want to test yourself to see if you are buoyant, someone else has to be watching you to see if the back of your head is out of the water.

1. Stand in chest-deep water.
2. Take a deep breath and hold it.
3. Lean forward, bending your knees, and let your feet rise up from the pool bottom. Let your arms float forward.
4. Relax all your muscles and let your arms and legs just hang at your sides. Float like a jellyfish.

The person you are with should look to see if the back of your head is out of the water. That means you have some buoyancy. Another way to know if you're buoyant —if you are alone—is to go to the side of the pool in chest-deep water. One hand holds the side of the pool and that arm is extended away from the side. Lean your head back with your ears in the water. Think of pushing your bellybutton towards the ceiling. Let your legs relax as much as possible, even if you have to wiggle them a little to come to the surface. Make sure your head is as far back in the water as it can go without putting your face in the water. Your ears have to be in the water. Breathe through your mouth and then make believe your are playing the piano with your hand holding the side of the pool. If you are still on top of the water, you have some buoyancy.

If you are not buoyant—and many people are not—the difference is people who aren't buoyant have to use more energy to stay on the surface of the water. (See finning the water on page 84). As we mentioned before, buoyant people have to use energy to stay **under** the surface of the water.

People who aren't buoyant who want to learn to swim may have to use flotation devices to help them learn.

When you are teaching this to a child, start by standing opposite the child holding the child's hands and doing the exercises. After the child is comfortable floating, then have the child try floating from the position of standing alone.

If your child can't stand in the water, your child can't recover. You can teach the child to float, but when the child recovers, he or she will need your support to be held up in the water.

If it seems impossible for your child to learn the Jellyfish Float, start with the Back Float instead.

You have to make sure that when you recover from the prone float or the back float that it's in a place where you can stand (the shallow end).

Without other skills, if you are in the deep end, you will sink.

If a child is vertical, and the child does not know how to tread water, the child needs a skill such as floating or long Doggy Paddle. If a child is horizontal the child has the opportunity to keep moving.

Jellyfish Float — How to teach yourself

Before trying this, read and practice the section on recovery.

1. Stand by the wall of the pool and hold the side or the gutter with one hand.
2. Take a deep breath and hold it. Put your face in the water and allow your legs to rise up.

When doing this, try to relax and feel the buoyancy of the water. When you need air, either lift your head, or bring your knees toward your chest, bring your feet to the bottom and stand. This builds confidence.

Back Float

The back float begins when your child feels the safest. This child is wearing a puddle jumper (a number 3 Coast Guard approved PFD.) She is confident in the PFD but she's not comfortable with floating on her back yet. With support from her parent and a teacher, she is allowing her ears to start to go in the water. That's the beginning of the back float. You can do this without the puddle jumper, but if your child needs the extra support, use one.

First show your child how you can float with your head back. Say, "Notice that my ears are in the water and I'm fine."

"I'm nice and relaxed. If I get all tense, I sink." Sink a little. Come up, and show and tell, "If I'm relaxed, I float."

"If I put my head back, my hips come up and I float."

"If I put my head up, and lift it out of the water, my hips go down and I sink." Show this. And tell it.

When that works well, you are ready for the next step.

The back float:

1. Stand in chest-deep water.
2. Take a deep breath and hold it (once you are floating, breathe through your mouth naturally.)
3. Bend your knees and lean backward, while putting your arms out to the sides.
4. Let your feet rise off the bottom of the pool.
5. Put your head back in the water, and submerge your ears. You are now floating.

If you have fear and can't relax enough to do this on your own, have someone stand behind you and support your shoulders under the water. You need very little support. The person can keep his or her hands under your shoulders through the whole process. If you're doing well, the person can support just your head. When you are lying in the water with the person's hands supporting your head, have the person slowly remove his or her hands.

Once you're on your back, breathe through your mouth. It helps you relax. The more relaxed you are, the more buoyant you are. The person who's helping you has things to say: "You're doing well. Keep your head in the water." Make believe you are pushing your belly-button toward the ceiling. Keep as much of your body in or under the water as you can.

With younger children, you can have the child put his or her head on your shoulder. Then have your cheek touch the child's cheek. That makes a child feel very safe.

(NOTE: If you're teaching a child, and you have beard stubble, the child may react negatively. Be sure to go in the pool smooth. A beard is soft. A shaved face is soft. But stubble doesn't work well.)

Then you can walk backwards with him or her. The drafting gives the child a little more buoyancy. Slowly let the child's head slip off your shoulder while you support the child's back and head with your chest and hand. Then only support the child's head.

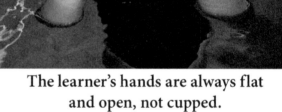

Then gradually, very slowly, let your hand drop away, and keep a hand gently on the child's chin.

While the child is drafting, the child is floating. You can constantly talk; "Push your belly button up. You're doing fine." Keep reminding the child in positive ways what's going on. "Breathe through your mouth. Keep your ears in the water. You're doing fine. Relax."

The learner's hands are always flat and open, not cupped.

You only have to do this a few seconds, then stop and try it another time.

If your child is having trouble with the back float, you can try two techniques to help. The first is called **finning** which is moving your hands 12 inches out with your thumbs down, and 12 inches back with your thumbs up. The movement is like spreading butter on bread. Practice this out of the pool first. Finning creates lift, like an airplane wing, with your hands. You tilt your hands a little (thumbs down and palms down), and move them out about 12 inches from the body, then tilt them, thumbs up, in.

The teacher has stepped out of the way, and tells the student, "You're floating on your own. Good job. Just relax. You're doing fine."

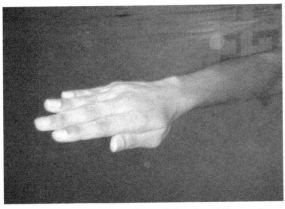

This is what your hand looks like when it's finning away from your body for floating. (This is a 17-year-old hand).

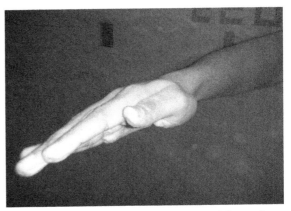

This is what your hand looks like when it's finning toward your body for floating.

In the pool, you stand at your child's head. The child is on his or her back. The child's hands should stay underwater. Your hands are supporting your child so the child doesn't sink. As the child starts to fin, the child will create lift. And you can start just by holding the child's head. Then you can draft, and start to move your hand from the back of the child's head to the chin.

If that doesn't work, we have another suggestion. This is called sculling. **Sculling** is similar to finning but you are drawing a figure 8 with your hands, sideways. You also practice this out of the pool first. If your child is too young, he or she may not yet have the coordination to do this. The child usually has to be older than five. It depends on how much time you spend practicing swimming. In the pool, like with finning, your child's hands are on her or his sides, palms down, in the water. The child's hands should stay underwater.

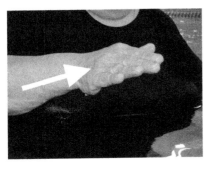

Sculling is a continuous motion in the water with both hands. Your hands are drawing a sideways figure 8.

If neither sculling nor finning works, try teaching the Elementary Backstroke. If your child does not have enough buoyancy, he or she will have to learn to move to stay on top of the water.

Back float practicing on your own. In the shallow end, stand next to the wall. Lay back, and let your feet come off the bottom. Let your arm (that is not holding onto the wall) stretch out under the water. Make believe there's a string attached to your belly button, pulling you up to the ceiling. Put your head back so your ears are in the water. Now, relax. Remember, you're holding the wall. As an adult, you want to try this first, so you can tell your child how it feels. (All these methods also work for adults teaching themselves to swim.)

Now, if you start to float, you want to gain a little more confidence. Take the hand holding the wall, or the edge of the pool, and pretend your are playing the piano with that hand.

This is what your hand looks like when it's pretending to play the piano.

This boy is about 6 years old. He's trying to learn to float on his own. He still has to learn to stick his other arm out in the water, but he's doing a great job. His ears are in the water and his legs are up high.

Why teaching recovery first is important

1. Recovering from the back float. First, reach down into the water as if reaching for a chair behind you. (This is an advanced teenaged swimmer. Do not compare your child to this example. It's for instruction purposes only. If your child can recover like this and the child is under five years old, please call us up. We want to meet the child.)

2. Recovering from the back float. Then bring your knees up. Your arms were behind you; start pulling them toward your sides. This will bring you more upright.

If a person does not know how to recover, the person becomes full of fear. The fear prevents floating. Or when the person is floating, the person can't stop floating. The person panics when trying to get out of the float position.

Recovery from the back float: Have someone standing with you to support you the first time you try this. To return to a standing position, reach with the palms of your hands, with your hands flat and open, down toward the bottom of the pool while you bend your knees and tuck your chin to your chest. This tilts you forward to a vertical position. This gesture is like pulling a chair from behind. You bring your hands forward, and then you do it again, as if you were jumping rope backward. Tilt your chin down. Straighten your legs, touch the pool bottom, and stand.

3. Recovering from the back float. Your feet are on the bottom. Your head is out of the water, and you have recovered from the back float. All you have to do is stand up.

Words of praise: "You're really getting the hang of this. I'm happy to see you working like this."

The more relaxed you are, the more buoyant you are. The more you practice, the better you float. If you can float, you will not panic in an emergency. You will have one more skill to fall back on. Floating makes the Elementary Back Stroke easier. Panicking is the leading cause of drowning. If you have a skill, you'll usually use it instead of panicking.

If a child has a skill, the child will almost always go to the skill instead of panicking. When a child learns to float, the child then knows a safe place to go in the water—to the back float position. Because your child's face will be out of the water, the child will be able to breathe, and if necessary, yell for help.

If the child succeeds say, "You were doing it all by yourself." Then move on to some other skill. Leaving on a positive note makes confidence grow.

Words of praise: "That's right!"

Practicing the Back Float on Your Own

If you are nervous about floating on your back, you can practice on your own and still be safe. This is for anyone who can stand in the low end of the pool. Go to chest-high water. Hold on to the side of the pool with one hand. Put your head back up to your ears in the water. Take a deep breath. Stretch your other arm out to the side. Relax as much as you can, knowing that you are holding the side of the pool. Let your feet rise from the bottom of the pool. You may have to do a little flutter kick to make that happen. Make believe you are relaxing in a reclining chair (as much as you can), and push your belly button toward the sky.

The teacher is letting the child's head rest on her chest. His ears are in the water. She is telling him to relax. She says, "You're doing fine. Push your belly button up toward the ceiling." Little by little he is starting to float on his own.

Another way to practice putting your ears in the water is to hug a kick board, lay back and start to relax. This will start to give you some confidence. You get used to putting your ears in the water—that is the most difficult thing for children.

Doggy Paddle

Doing the Doggy Paddle involves moving your arms the same way dogs move their paws when they swim. This is one of the first swimming strokes that we suggest you teach your child (If this does not work, we suggest you go to the section about Elementary Backstroke; see the Index.) The Doggy Paddle uses the three essential skills that you have to use to swim. The three essential skills are breathing, moving your arms, and kicking your feet.

To practice these skills with children, some swim teachers put new words to the tune for the song, "If You're Happy and You Know It." If you don't know the song, you can find the tune for it on the Internet. Singing the (modified) song helps teach these skills. After the first time you sing, "If you're happy and you know it, blow some bubbles," everybody blows bubbles. As the child gets more advanced, the child puts her face lower in the water. The second time, the child sings, "If you're happy and you know it, paddle your arms," the adult and the child paddle their arms. The third time they sing the words, "If you're happy and you know it, kick your feet," they kick their feet. (See the Index under Songs for more information.)

The Mechanics of the Doggy Paddle

The mother is supporting her child at her side. She is reinforcing the instructions by repeating, "Reach out and pull down. Reach out and pull down." This is a swimming readiness skill. The child still does not have flat hands. She is swimming with her hands in fists. This is the beginning of learning this stroke. Mom makes sure to give continuous positive feedback, "You're the best at this!"

With practice comes improvement. Mom is only holding the back of her PFD. The child's hands are flatter. She's reaching out farther. So, she's doing the long Doggy Paddle now. Her mother says to her, "I am so proud of you!"

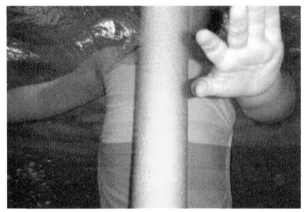

This is a supervised skill. Her parent is right next to her to support her as needed. The child is sitting on the floating foam noodle like she would sit on a horse, which holds her head above water. This turns learning into a game. She's doing the long Doggy Paddle on each side of the noodle.

This child is using the long Doggy Paddle and kicking. Her head is out of the water. The instructor is giving her a little support only when she needs, by putting a hand under her tummy.

This is a teenager on a swimming team. We're showing this photograph because this is a perfect example of how long Doggy Paddle should look underwater, but for clarity, she's demonstrating above the water.

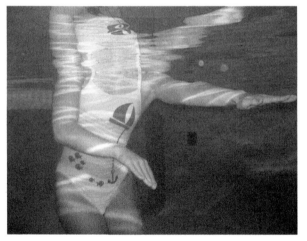

This is an experienced swimmer showing what the long Doggy Paddle should look like underwater.

It's a good idea to practice this with your child first while standing on dry land.

The most important part of this stroke is the positioning of the hands. (See photos above for images of correct hand positions.) Your hands should always be flat and open as in all swimming stokes. The water will be displaced by the palms of your hands—this means you will be pushing the water with the palms of your hands. Your palms should also be facing down. In the elementary part of this stroke, you demonstrate, and then just say to the child "paddle your arms." Any effort your child makes toward this is acceptable. However, as your child's skills and dexterity become more advanced, you want to help refine the stroke. You want to tell the child to "reach and dig." By this we mean the child wants to send his fingers as far as the child can in front of him. When your child's arms are extended and elbows are straight, then tell your child to "reach and pull down" with one arm and then the other. This takes some coordination. It's a good idea for you to demonstrate, practice on dry land, and then try it in the pool.

In the beginning it looks like a dog paddling because the stroke is much shorter. Later, as the child learns the stroke and the stroke starts to hold the child up in the water, the child can take longer strokes, and start to go a little bit slower. Words of praise: "That's astounding!"

This skill can be also be practiced out of the pool, sitting on the edge of the pool or even on your sofa in the living room. Sometimes when you demonstrate out of the water, it's easier for your child to mimic or imitate you and learn.

For a child who wants to practice who can stand or walk in the low end, have the child walk in the shallow end and lower herself or himself into the water until it's up to the tops of your child's shoulders (so your child's head is above the water).

If your child feels fear, stand in the water facing your child. Put your hands out palms up. Have the child put his or her hands on your palms. Tell your child to kick his or her feet. You walk backwards as the child kicks the feet. This creates a draft which helps support the child in the water. Don't walk toward the deep end or the shallow end because you will run out of space. Instead go side-to-side or if you're in a round pool, circle.

Tell the child to do the arm motions of the Doggy Paddle. With your hands, do the reverse motions. Say, "Reach and pull down," and demonstrate this. Praise, "Look, you're doing very well." If your child seems confident or is enjoying it (enjoyment is also confidence), say, "Now we're going to try it with one hand, and I'm going to pull away a hand." Let the child do the Doggy Paddle with one arm, and you support his other arm. Don't overdo it. That's enough for one lesson.

Some people try to have a child learn to swim in one day. If you press for that, you could have a setback.

Another way of teaching practicing two skills at the same time: Kicking and Moving your Arms

This is a good practice technique for children who are not tall enough to stand in the pool.

A good way to practice is to have your child learn without knowing he is learning. You can do this by having your child jump in with you there to catch them.

Jumping in with parental support is fun and builds confidence.

Notice how much fun the parent is having.

This child still needs support in the water, so she's wearing a puddle jumper. She can still learn to kick and paddle her arms while wearing the PFD, and have fun at the same time.

Jumping in is a lot of fun. See the Index for more information. Remember before a child jumps, he or she should always have his or her toes over the edge of the pool. (If this is an above-ground pool, the child can't stand or sit on the edge. You can practice this on one of the lowest steps of the ladder — not the top step, but the one below it entering the pool). If the child is less skilled, catch your child as soon as he or she enters the water, turn the child around and support his or her going to the ladder or the edge of the pool in the side-to-side position. Then say, "Paddle your arms and kick your feet! Wonderful job!"

If your child has more skill (if your child is comfortable putting his or her head underwater), step back a few feet, tell your child to bend his or her knees, and jump towards you. As soon as the child goes underwater, pick the child up under the armpits and look at her or him in the face-to-face position. Say "Great job! You did it!" Now, if the child smiles, you turn the child around, support the child and say, "Kick your feet and paddle your arms." As the child swims back to the wall, you release the child. If the child sinks, support the child again until he or she gets back to the wall. If the child is able to make it back to the wall with a little push from the side-to-side position, going the three-to-five feet, then the next time, move back another foot or so from the wall or the ladder. You CATCH the child at the same distance as before, and then next time you take a few steps back after you catch the child.

Of course, always attend to your child. Even if your child can swim across the pool, the child is safer wearing a #2 or #3 Coast Guard certified PFD.

If the child is tall enough to stand in the water, the child can put his or her feet on the wall and push off and start to kick feet and paddle arms (see photographs on next few pages).

To Practice Blowing bubbles and Moving Your Arms

When your child can do the arm movements, have the child add blowing bubbles to the arm movements. You can say to the child, "One arm, blow bubbles, one arm take a breath; one arm blow bubbles, one arm take a breath."

Have your child walk in the shallow end. The water should be up to her neck. Her hands should be flat and open. She should shoot her fingers out and pull down hard. This is the long Doggy Paddle.

If your child is getting a little frustrated, take a break and play with blowing a ping-pong ball. Tell her to move her arms the same way and blow the ping-pong ball. Tell her not to touch the ping-pong ball, just blow on it. You and the child could race, if you have two ping-pong balls. Let your child win. Make yourself the fool. Tell your child how well she is are doing.

If your child can do the Doggy Paddle and kick, the child is ready to put his or her head in the water. This is a most challenging moment for a child!

Review the section about kicking and blowing bubbles (see Index).

Explain to your child why this is worth doing: you get to move forward faster. When your child is blowing bubbles with her head in the water, her hips will be a little higher. Then she reaches and digs with her arms. And when kicking with her feet, she is swimming and will be getting forward momentum. Demonstrate this for the child.

Next try doing the long Doggy Paddle with a little assistance. Put your hand under the child's stomach and help her until you feel she is swimming on her own.

A good way to do this is have your child kick and blow bubbles.

Pushing off the wall in the prone position

This is how it looks on the surface. Some people may have problems putting the face in the water and may wait for the very last moment.

Hold the wall with one hand. Put the other hand in front of you, and put your feet up on the wall so you can push off.

When you release the wall with your hand, bring the hand that was holding the wall to meet the other hand. Both arms are in front of you with your hands touching. Then push off the wall and glide.

After she pushes off the wall, notice how nicely her hands are together.

She is staying in the glide position and kicking her feet. She's not going to pick up her head until she expels all her air and she touches the rope. It's about eight yards. Some kids stop in the middle. Make sure you're there to catch your child.

This push-off-the-wall-and-glide technique is done on your stomach. Demonstrate this for your child before teaching your child how to do it. If your child has a problem with this, go to teaching the Elementary Backstroke (see Index). Five minutes later, you can come back to this stroke.

The child faces you when she pushes off the wall. The child reaches back and holds the wall with her "best" hand. This hand is probably the one with which your child opens doors.

The child puts her feet up flush against the wall and stretches the other arm straight out towards you in the water.

You're there to catch your child, one to two feet away. Tell your child, "When releasing the other hand from the wall, put it next to the hand that's out front." Then tell your child, "You will fly like Superman (or Catwoman) and then I will catch you."

As your child pushes off the wall with her feet, she should put her head in the water and blow bubbles. (You will demonstrate this first.) Allow your child to glide out to you. Catch your child's hands. Your child won't do this unless she trusts you. And you must catch your child.

Then give positive reinforcement, "You're the best! Good going!" As your child gains confidence, go three to four feet away and then further. As you get further out, you can encourage your child, "Kick your feet!" This helps your child with forward momentum. Do not let your child sink under the water. It would be a step backward. If your child is not very confident, hold your child's hands and help her glide ... pull her along.

Then say, "Let's see how far you can go on one breath of air." Eventually, the more advanced child will want to have one hand on top of the other as the child pushes off. It improves the glide.

When your child can do this pretty well and with confidence

After your child does the Doggy Paddle with her head out of the water, ask your child to do the Doggy Paddle with her head in the water blowing bubbles. The child can push off the wall and start doing the Doggy Paddle. After your child pushes off the wall, she has been expelling all her air. Instead of stopping and standing, or your catching her, ask your child, "Try to pick up your head for air and then Doggy Paddle and see what happens." When the child picks up her head, the child gets as much air as possible, and then goes back to blowing bubbles and swimming the long Doggy Paddle and kicking. When the child is blowing bubbles, the child's whole face should be in the water (See the Index for blowing bubbles).

In the beginning your child may not put her whole face in the water while blowing bubbles. You can encourage the child by saying, "The more of your head is in the water, the better you'll swim." The child is much less likely to sink. As the Red Cross says, "Think, so you don't sink."

After your child has had practice putting her face in the water and blowing some bubbles, now teach the child how to kick. You want her to learn to keep her feet in the water, but as close to the surface as possible. She should be able to hear her feet splash. Mike says, "This is a test. Is it easier to kick with your head out of the water or is it easier to kick and blow bubbles with your head in the water?"

Once your child can kick and blow bubbles well at the wall, it's time to start doing it in the water. When you're not holding the wall, it's much easier to kick and blow bubbles. Instead your child can hold a juice container.

If she finds it easier to blow bubbles and kick with her head in the water than to do so with her head out of the water, that's a good sign.

If you don't have a kick board, you can use an empty half-gallon juice container with the cap on it as a kick board.

If the child is kicking and gets tired. He can take a rest by stopping and holding on to the container for buoyancy.

You, the adult, can assist the child. This is a way to show the child that when she puts her face in the water and blows bubbles, her feet are higher in the water and it's easier to kick. Tell the child, "I'm going to put my hand under your tummy. This way you know you won't sink. I want you to put your face in the water and blow bubbles. You'll see that your feet come up higher and you'll kick more easily." Put your hand lightly beneath the child's stomach so she has a little more confidence. Children can fear doing anything. If they know you are holding them they'll have less fear. Many children accomplish this betwen four and five. How fast they progress depends on individual differences and how much time the child spends in the pool with you.

This girl has learned to blow bubbles and kick her feet. Now she's practicing turning her head to get air. This is the beginning of Freestyle or Crawl.

Show and tell: In this challenging moment, the child has to have something to fall back on instead of panicking. If your child has any frustration or difficulty at all, and she is tall enough to stand in the shallow end, remind her, "You can stand." You can also stop at this point, and go right to teaching the Elementary Backstroke. Come back later. Have other things ready to teach. You have to be flexible in order to be an effective teacher, and make this experience good for your child.

When your child gets to the point where she has all those skills—breathing, moving arms, kicking feet, and she is moving forward—HURRAY, YOUR CHILD IS SWIMMING! Say, "You did it. You're swimming!" Congratulate yourself as well. This is a very special time. Enjoy it. Pat yourself on the back. You have done it. And there is still a long way to go.

Pushing off the wall on your back.

This is what it looks like underwater.

Start by having your child hold the side of the pool and put her feet up on the wall.

Have your child lay her head back into the water. Then the child should release her hands, and push with her feet gently. If your child pushes too hard, her head goes underwater. Have your child put her arms at her sides.

The child's head slides down the parent's chest, and the parent is walking backward, drafting the child. The child knows she's pushed too hard off the wall if her face goes underwater. Also, if she does not tilt her head back enough, her face will go underwater. Tell the child, "Look at me." That usually puts the child's head in the perfect position.

The child glides backwards, but your role as a parent is to walk backward and draft the child. The parent's hands support the child's back. Your hands just touch your child's back, there is no need to push upward. The parent also reminds the child, "Put your ears in the water." The child should have already practiced putting her ears in the water. See the Index for more information.

As the child glides away from the wall, the child starts to kick. (If you are doing this while teaching your child, stand behind her and walk backwards. That gives her lift, because you're drafting. And it gives extra confidence. If your child's head starts to go under, lift it with your hand and say, "You did everything perfectly, but next time we're going to push a little easier.")

Tell your child: "Start to kick." As long as your child's head is back in the water and the child is kicking, almost everyone can do this. Tell your child: "Keep your arms at your sides, or they will slow you down."

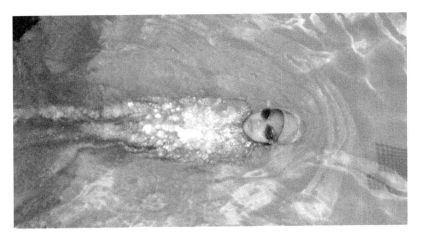

Now the child is doing this on her own. With confidence.

This push-off-the-wall technique is also used later for the Elementary Backstroke, and the racing Backstroke.

To demonstrate pushing off the wall on your back: Start by standing in the pool facing the wall—preferably with a lip or gutter where you can hang on. Grasp the edge of the pool or the gutter with two hands, bending your legs, and placing your feet on the wall. Lean back and put the back of your head in the water. (Do not push off too hard. That would bring your head underwater. Here we are trying to keep your face out of the water.) Let go with your hands and leave them at your sides, as you float back and push off the wall with your feet and legs.

Have your child hold the edge of the pool with her hands. Then have her place the balls of her feet up against the side of the pool. You stand a few feet behind your child near her head.

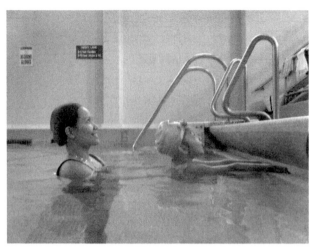

Move back so that your child can release her arms from the wall.

Catch your child with your hands supporting the child's back. Put her head on your shoulder so she can hear you.

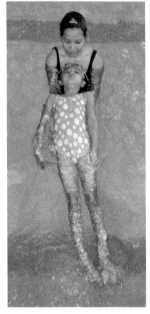

Tell your child, "Kick your feet, and put your ears in the water, and look at me." Let your child's head slip from your shoulder into the water. You are still supporting her back with your hands if necessary.

As your child starts to kick her feet, you release your hands and walk backwards. This creates drafting. Your child comes along with you. This will build confidence.

After practicing for awhile, your child should be able to do this on her own.

Be ready to support her as needed after she pushes off the wall. Tell your child, "Lay your head back, let go with your hands first. Leave your arms and hands at your side." As the child drifts back, tell her, "Push off the wall with your feet." As soon as your child is gliding toward you, say, "Kick your feet."

The first time your child does this skill, stand behind your child and catch her quickly, before she sinks. If your child is moving well on top of the water, proceed backwards. That will cause drafting. As long as your child is gliding toward you on the surface of the water, you keep moving backwards, causing drafting. You are ready to support your child before she sinks.

Give positive feedback for any attempt, "Good job!" and try again. On the next attempt, step back a foot or two and have your child glide on her own a little bit further. Say, "Kick your feet." Then catch your child, or when your child slows, support her by holding her up under her shoulders, and give your child positive feedback. "Well, look at you go!"

Children who are fearful need support right away. As soon as the child lays back in the water, allow her head to touch your body. As you walk backward, your body will cause drafting, which allows your child to stay afloat in the water. As the child gets better at this, move your body away from her body a little more. There will be less drafting and more skill involved. Children who are not fearful will need support later in the process. Say, "Do that until I catch you." Repeat until your child is confident with pushing off the wall and kicking. See how far your child can get with just kicking. Some children can go pretty far.

Push off the wall for Elementary Backstroke
Push off the wall and glide.

When first learning the Elementary Backstroke, start by pushing off the wall. This will give your child lift and help him or her learn this stroke more easily. Your child must also be able to put his or her head back in the water. This means that your child's ears will be getting wet. (See the Index for information about putting your head in the water.)

This skill helps your child improve his or her learning ability. When your child pushes off the wall and glides, your child has momentum that creates lift.

Hold the edge of the pool. Put your feet up on the side of the pool. Get ready to let go of the side of the pool and lay your head back in the water.

After you let go of the wall and put your head back in the water, gently push your legs off the wall. Keep your arms at your sides. Start your glide.

Start kicking your feet. That will keep you moving. The movement will keep you gliding.

Safety moves to teach your child: The Elementary Backstroke

The Elementary Backstroke is probably the most important stroke you can teach your child, both for relaxation and survival. If you can teach your child how to float or your child has already learned how, then this is a good next step. (See the Index for instructions about teaching your child to float.) In lieu of learning how to float first, the child can learn to stay up by doing this stroke and moving her arms first. Then she learns to stay on the surface of the water and may learn to float later.

Teach this first because most people can learn this stroke, even people who aren't buoyant. It's leisurely. Most people can do this stroke with just the arm movements. Leg movements help, but they are not necessary to do the stroke. (We talk about the leg movements much later in the book. See the Index for more information.)

In an emergency, if your child has an emergency plan, your child will probably use it. The skills "kick in." Your child won't panic, and your child will save her own life. The Elementary Backstroke can be part of your child's "emergency plan." Your child can do this with a PFD on or off. Tell your child that it's also called a "survival stroke," meaning that in an emergency situation your training kicks in. You have a choice: Do you want to panic in the water, or roll over on your back and do this stroke?

Teach this stroke first because the children get to be on their backs. It's easier for the child to breathe whenever the child wants, with his or her face out of the water. So this eliminates one of the things the child has to remember to stay afloat. Even if children aren't that buoyant, they can still—when they move their arms in the Elementary Backstroke—stay on the surface. Movement pushes a swimmer up. The buoyancy gives your child confidence, and it's fun when children first feel like they are "flying" or swimming in the water. The kids get excited.

If a child fears the water, you can teach this one skill. When he or she is able to do this, then you can teach other skills without causing fear, because the child now has a skill to fall back on. *Always remember to remove the fear and then introduce the skill.*

Under certain conditions, the Elementary Backstroke saves energy. You use this stroke if you're wearing a Personal Flotation Device (PFD). This is why we call it a survival stroke. If you try to swim Freestyle or in the prone position while wearing a life jacket you will use too much energy. Doing the Elementary Backstroke helps conserve heat in your body which helps prevent hypothermia in an emergency situation.

It's also relatively easy for parents to teach, once you get the "soldier, chicken, airplane" concept.

The Elementary Backstroke is a not a great stroke for exercise or swimming laps.

Teach this out of the water first.
You can practice this at home, before you go to the pool. This will allow your child to be familiar and comfortable with the body motions. First practice this skill standing up. Then have your child practice while lying on the ground. Rehearse at the pool also. You and your child can practice the arm movements while standing by the pool.

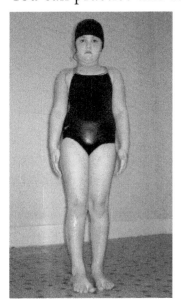

For younger children, tell them to start out in "soldier" position.

The child moves her arms up her sides very slowly to the "chicken" or "monkey" position. If the child chooses the chicken position, you can say, "Bok bok bok," like a chicken does.

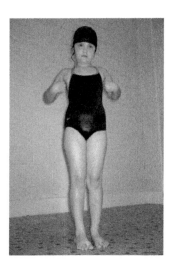

Remember to have fun when you're demonstrating this to your children. For example, you can say, "Gobble gobble gobble gobble. Is that the sound of a chicken?" And they will tell you no, it's a turkey. Then show them how a chicken moves its wings and say, "Bok bok bok." The child will enjoy watching your demonstration. She will want to mimic you or want to show you how much better she can do it than you can. Always give your child positive feedback and compliment her on her effort. "Great chicken!"

We use a saying to help children remember the complete arm movement. The saying is, "Soldier, chicken, T," or "Soldier, monkey, airplane." Use the words you're more comfortable using. You can also get creative and make up your own saying.

Have your child stand on the deck, with arms spread out and fingers at the height of the ears. Explain that this is the "airplane" or "T" position. Call it whichever you think would be easier for your child to remember. Your child should have her palms down.

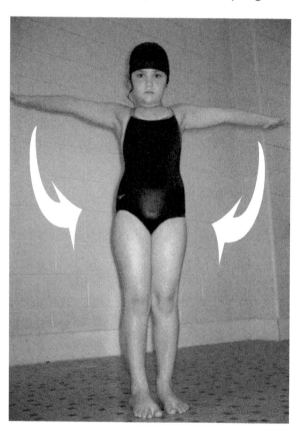

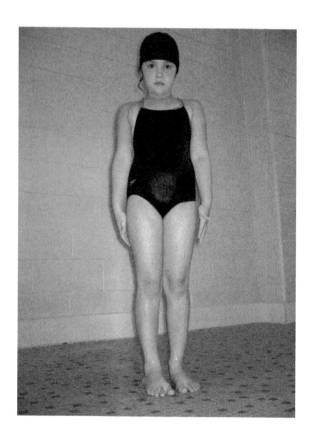

Everything is done slowly until the T position. This is the power part of the stroke.

When your child goes back to soldier position, she pushes her hands down in the water hard, and leaves her hands at her sides for a second to feel the glide. Remember, the head should be back in the water. Repeat.

Teach the arm movements one at a time.

This is a more advanced swimmer, showing much better technique. This is for the parent's reference only. It is a series of photographs of what the Elementary Backstroke arm movements look like when an advanced swimmer does them well.

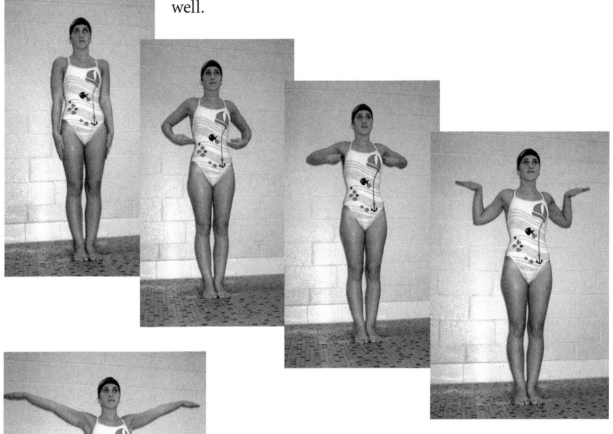

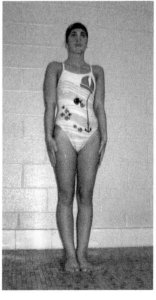

1. Show your child how to stand at attention. Stand with your arms resting at the sides of your body. Have your child try it. Tell your child that this is the "soldier position."

This child is in soldier position.

This child is going from soldier position towards chicken...

This child is also sliding her hands toward the chicken position.

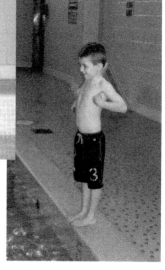

This child is at the chicken position. "Bok bok bok."

2. Then have your child slide his or her fingertips VERY SLOWLY up the sides of the body to where the fingertips almost touch the armpits. This is called the "chicken" or "monkey" position. Try not to let the child's hands or arms come out of the water. Demonstrate wiggling your arms like a chicken. Remember, this is about having fun; have the child wiggle his or her arms like a chicken.

When the child extends the arms from the chicken to the airplane position, GO SLOW, and keep the hands in the water as much as possible. He or she should first put the palms down and then shoot the fingertips out toward the sides.

3. Then say, "T." Have the child extend his or her arms to look like the letter "T" or like an airplane. The arms should be at the height of the ears, palms down.

Now the child is ready to learn the next part of the stroke, which is the power phase. Putting the movements together gives the child the momentum to move in water. Demonstrate the connected motions as one fluid group by saying, "soldier," "chicken," "airplane," while you stand on deck and do the motions. When you go from "T" to "Soldier," have the child return to soldier position by pushing his or her arms down to the sides. The child can move faster here. It's important to keep the palms of the hands down when doing this part of the stroke, and the elbows straight. The child should keep her or his arms straight. (See page 110 to fine tune the details of hand positions. Our purpose here is to give the child the basics of a safety stroke to fall back on.) When your child goes from "airplane" to "soldier" position, remind your child to imagine that he or she is pushing water with the palms of his or her hands flat and open. The palms of the hands should always push water toward the feet. The arms do not come out of the water.

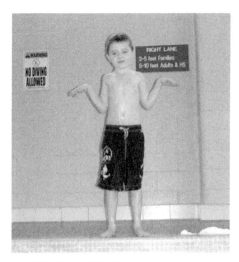

This child is on his way to the T position.

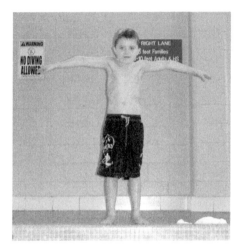

This child is in the T position.

Now the child is back to Soldier position. When he does this in the water—coming back to Soldier position—he glides for a few seconds before repeating the sequence. He remembers that "Soldier, Chicken, T," are done very slowly. Hands do not come out of the water. When you go from T position back to Soldier, your palms go down toward your feet and you push hard to get back to the Soldier position.

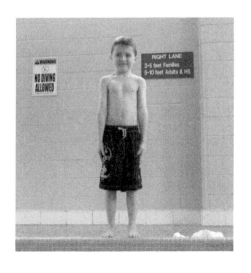

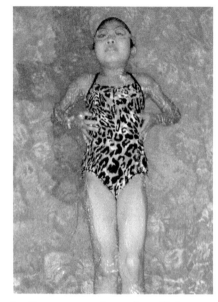

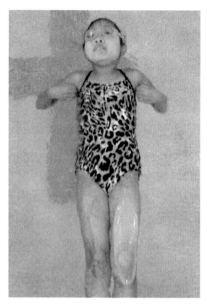

1. This is how the Elementary Backstroke is done in the water. This is the soldier position. The child's head goes back. The ears go in the water, and the arms go at your sides.

2. Let your hands slide up your body and go into the chicken position.

3. This is the chicken position.

5. This is a perfect T.

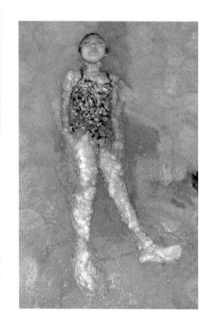

4. This is going to the T position. Shoot finger tips straight out until arms are straight. Palms should be the same height as ears. Palms should be facing down toward feet. This leads you to the T position.

6. Going back to Soldier position. Notice that her head is back in the water. Palms are facing her feet. She should pull her hands down hard from the T position.

7. Now she is in glide position, kicking her feet with a regular flutter kick. She's about to start moving her hands back up her body to go into the chicken position.

When the child can do this on land, it's time to try it in the water. If your child doesn't want to try this, don't push. You and your child can practice this at home on the living room floor until your child is comfortable. Doing this on the floor teaches you to keep your arms level. They don't go up or down. They stay at the side of your body.

If your child has fears about putting her head back in the water, see the Index for how to teach this skill. Tell your child, "It's very hard to float on your back without your ears in the water. You have to put the back of your head all the way in the water. If you don't, your hips sink." Demonstrate this. Say, "It feels funny with your ears in the water, but you get used to it." If you want to practice this you can put your own head back and first put one ear in the water, and then the other, and then put both ears in the water. Show the child how first, then ask the child to try it.

You can also trying putting an adult's silicone swim cap on your child so it covers your child's ears. (We only suggest silicon, not any other kind of cap. Silicon keeps the head warmer, and it can help keep water out of your child's ears.) Then when you child puts his or her head back, it covers the ears. Even if water goes in, it can go so gently it does not seem to bother the child. It feels like someone is covering the child's ears with a pair of hands.

Children often fear getting their faces wet. Reassure your child, "I promise you your face won't get wet." Keep your promise. If for any reason you goof, acknowledge that you made a mistake and tell your child you'll do your best not to do it again.

If you find that you're continually flustering or frightening your child, have your child practice this stroke with a PFD on. It's a good way for a child to gain confidence while learning this stroke.

If your child is still not happy in the water with you, it might be worth doubling your effort to find a certified class where your child can learn... Or hire a certified instructor to give your child a few lessons. Sometimes children learn better from someone else than they do from Mom or Dad. We assume though, that this won't happen, so let us continue.

This child is going to the T position. Shoot your finger tips straight out until your arms are straight. Your palms should be the same height as your ears. Your palms should be facing down toward your feet. This leads you to the T position.

When you first train your child to do this in the water, stand behind your child's head. With both your hands, gently support your child's head. If he or she is small enough, you can also support the back. Walk backwards. Drafting helps. You cannot both support the child and stand at the child's side with this stroke.

The support gives your child an essential sense of security while first practicing the stroke in the water.

Soldier

If your child is afraid to put her ears back in the water, you may want to start by keeping her head a little higher on your chest, and then gently start lowering her ears into the water. Say, "It's OK. It's OK." Walk backward and let her feel the water slowly. This may take some time.

Notice the eye contact, and the arms pushing down. The eye contact is good because that means the child's head is back far enough.

Chicken or Monkey

T position or Airplane Position. Her palms are down, her head is back, her hands are at her ears… She's ready to go to the "power phase" back to soldier position.

Back to soldier, and glide.

~~ SPLASH ~~

Ask your child to hold the wall while facing it, and then gently push off. It's very important to let go of the wall easily, lay back and then push back gently. Pushing too hard will cause the child's head to go underwater.

When the child is in a floating position on the back, and you are supporting the child, start to move slowly backwards. Keep slowly repeating, "Soldier, Chicken, T." Have the child say it with you. The backward movement that you make will give the child some lift which gives the child a little more buoyancy. It also creates a draft in the water that actually pulls her or him along. Support your child's head so your child can breathe. As necessary, gently remind your child, "Put your head back. Look at me. Breathe. Soldier. Chicken. Airplane." Remind your child, "No splashing. Your arms stay in the water. Do it slow." When the child's hands are in the water, he or she tends to float better.

After a few times, if your child seems very comfortable with this stroke, you can gradually support the child's head with only one hand.

Tell the child to straighten her legs like she's doing a jumping jack. Do this slowly, too.

This is the proper leg movement for the Elementary Backstroke (the children remember this as soldier-chicken-T). The first step is have the child put her head on the parent's shoulder. Hold her in a secure position. Dad's hands are under her arms, and her cheek is by his cheek. Tell the child to pick her knees up. The parent walks backwards and is drafting. Do this slowly.

From the jumping jack position, the child keeps her legs straight and brings her feet together fast. This propels her in the water.

Then, after your child gets very comfortable with that, you can let go of your child's head, while remaining very close.

Praise your child, "Excellent!" This takes some practice. Be patient.

Elementary Backstroke flutter kick

For more advanced children who have learned this skill, we suggest teaching them the leg movements. The elementary leg movement is the flutter kick. This is an up-and-down kick used in Backstroke, Freestyle, and other things you can teach later. (See the Index for more information.)

Look at the child kicking and give her or him corrective feedback as needed, such as, "Don't bend your knees so much. Point your toes. Don't kick so hard." Remember to give positive feedback, "Excellent job, much better. Wonderful." Children can also practice this kick while hugging a kickboard or a noodle or while wearing a PFD. Her feet should not go more than twelve inches apart. They should not splash too much. The big toes should go back and forth within a few inches of each other.

If your child does anything similar to this and the hips stay up high in the water, and the legs do not sink, this is acceptable.

Elementary Backstroke: Adding Breathing

You can tell your child, "Swimming this stroke is like juggling because you have to do several things at once. You have to do your soldier-chicken-airplane, you have to breathe, and you have to kick. Now it's time to practice coordination."

Demonstrate the stroke for your child and say, "When going from airplane to soldier I push down fast and I breathe in fast." (Parents: That's the power phase.)

"Then I wait a few seconds while I glide, before going back to chicken."

"I breathe out slowly from the soldier to chicken to airplane position and I also move slowly." (Parents: If you move too fast, your head will go underwater.)

"I kick just a little. Little flutter kicks. My head is always back." (Parents: the ears have to be in the water or the legs will drop too low and the child will start to sink.) Ask your child if there are any questions.

The flutter kick helps hold up the legs; and the ears in the water help hold up the hips. As your child practices this, he or she will be able to do this with more confidence. If this is not your stroke, start with the long Doggy Paddle instead.

Often a child will try to move fast or kick hard. You can say, "You don't have to try so hard. Go nice and slow." When we teach this in class, after eight 45-minute group lessons, if the child can go all the way across the pool using the elementary back stroke, that is very good progress. Words of praise: "Good thinking. That's it."

After this practice is a good time to sing, "If you're happy and you know it." See the Index under Songs for revised lyrics suitable for learning swimming.

Mike says, "When a kid gets really confident, and he or she wants to show me how much they know, I'll say, 'OK, I'm going to push you in the water like you fell off the side, and I want to see you float and do the Elementary Backstroke.' I always let them know what I'm going to do, and I do it with their consent. They're dying to show it to me. They'll do it. And when they float, it means that if they ever fall in a pool, they'll have a skill to fall back on. Their training will likely kick right in. They'll probably go right into a float, or bobbing. We're giving them a skill. They will almost always use the skill instead of panicking." Words of praise: "Well, look at you go!"

Easy Elementary Backstroke

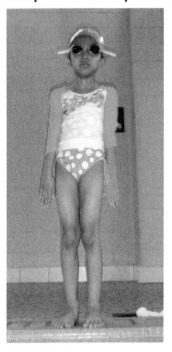

There is another way to help your child stay afloat in the water on her back, if the Elementary Backstroke is too difficult. It's not as efficient as the Elementary Backstroke but it can work. And it may be a little simpler. It's called "Karate chop out! Push in!"

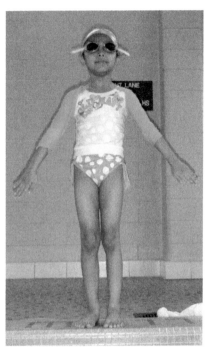 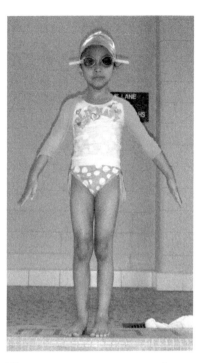

Practice this on deck first. You are standing up, but pretending you are on your back. Your hands are flat.

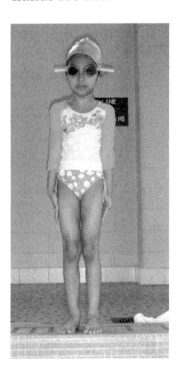

Make believe you are doing a karate chop motion with your hands. Your palms now face behind you (in the water they would be facing down toward the bottom of the pool). This motion is done slowly underwater.

Your arms go out about 45 degrees, then you turn palms in toward your body and bring them in fast.

Your hands come in fast to your sides. This pushes your body through the water. Repeat.

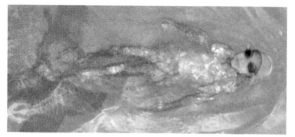
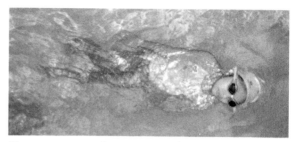

In the water, you're on your back. Your ears are in the water. You're kicking your feet. Your hands are flat at your sides. You turn your palms towards the bottom of the pool. Slowly karate chop out 45°.

Turn your palms toward your body and push in hard.

Repeat.

This is a truncated form of the Elementary Backstroke and sometimes is easier for the child to understand and put into practice. This section shows the child how to do the arm movements for the easy Elementary Backstroke. This eventually leads to the child being able to do the real Elementary Backstroke: Soldier, chicken, T.

You're supporting your child. Her head is on your chest and your palms supporting your child's back. Your child's hands are at her side, palms down.

Your child moves her arms underwater like a slow-motion karate chop outward. Her elbows should be straight. Her arms should stop at about a 45° angle away from her body.

Now she turns her palms inward toward her body. Her hands are always open and flat. She pushes her palms toward her body fast and hard. This is the power part of the stroke.

She returns her hands to the start position. Now she turns her hands back to the karate chop position and repeats. The parent is holding the child so she can practice the arm strokes in the water.

Rolling Over

Once your child knows the Elementary Backstroke and one prone position stroke, you can try teaching rolling over.

Rolling over is an important skill. You can start to introduce this skill when your child is at the infant pre-school level. It can be fully learned by older children who can swim two different strokes—a stroke on their back and on their stomach—such as the Elementary Backstroke, and the Doggy Paddle or the Breast Stroke.

This is a good skill for your child to learn because rolling over allows your child to go from one style of swimming to another. Infants can learn what it feels like to roll over from the prone position to the back floating position with our assistance. As the child improves, the child learns to roll over on his or her own. This is a good skill to teach your child because it is useful in the teaching process: it helps eliminate fear. When your child is learning the basic swim skills—Doggy Paddle and Elementary Backstroke—if the child knows how to roll over, if the child starts to panic or get tired, he or she can roll over into the stroke that's comfortable to do. It gives children confidence to learn a new skill and have something to fall back on. Knowing how to roll over helps with that.

Rolling over for toddlers.

Toddlers need your assistance. Rolling over is a swimming readiness skill. The child is aware of rolling over but you always help your child. It requires some dexterity and practice.

The child rolls over from front to back. Start from the side-to-side position. (See page 64 for details.) Make sure your child's face stays out of the water. While you walk forward, you say, "Blow bubbles, kick your feet." You should be deep down, so your arms are in the water. When you are ready to do the rollover, bend your knees. You roll your child as you start to turn. You walk in front of your child while holding him in the side-to-side position. In this side-to-side position, your arms should be closer to the child's armpits. This way, when you start your roll, you will finish with your arms close to the armpits.

You say, "Now we're going to roll over." Say to your child, **"Now your belly button is going from the water to the air. We're going to roll over."** You then roll the child onto his back, working your hands up to the armpits. You pull the child back towards you into a back float position. Say, "It's OK, just relax and put your ears in the water." Your child's head is just touching your chest. You're now walking backward, drafting your child so the child will feel the buoyancy of the water. Support your child from under the armpits. Move to one hand under the head and one under the back. Or use your body to support the child's head and keep both hands under the child. While your child is moving along with you, if you feel the child has some buoyancy, remove your hand from the child's back and just support the head.

If you see your child is uncomfortable, stop. Infant/pre-school aquatics are about joy. If they are not joyful, you—the adult—need to learn to teach correctly.

More Advanced Rolling Over

Rolling over front to back. She's rolling from the prone position to her back. You lift one arm out of the water and push the other arm down. That turns you over. From the back position to the prone position, you also lift one arm out of the water and push the other arm down. This automatically rolls you over.

This is for children who are tall enough to stand in the shallow end, and are able to do at least one of the strokes (the long Doggy Paddle, the Elementary Backstroke or the Breast Stroke) with some confidence. To demonstrate how to roll over: Stand in the shallow end of the pool. Float on your back or stomach. Lift one arm out of the water and push the other arm down into the water. This should automatically roll you over.

Then have your child stand in the shallow end of the pool. Have the child float on her back or stomach (jellyfish float). Tell her to lift one arm up out of the water and push one arm down into the water. This will automatically roll her over. Stand at your child's head, and if the child starts to panic, support her by saying, "It's OK, recover." If she needs assistance to recover, put your hands underneath her and help her (See pages 79 and 87 for instructions about recovery).

When your child can do this in the low end of the pool, she is ready to push off the wall in the low end, in the prone position with her arms out in front of her like Superman flying. She can also glide out on her back with her arms out to her side, face out, head back into the water. When she feels far from the wall, she can lift one arm out of the water and push one arm down. This should roll the child over.

Now, if she has a problem while swimming, she will know how to roll over and go to a skill she knows and feels comfortable with. She can then swim to safety. This is why rolling over is important.

Always start with the swimming stroke the child is less confident with so that the child can roll into a stroke with which he or she is more confident.

Many people are afraid to swim toward the deep end. Respect this. If you're in a pool with a shallow and deep end, always have your child swim toward the shallow end. This will also build confidence. The child will know he or she is swimming to a place the child can stand. The child can also can swim toward the side of the pool.

If your child is doing the Elementary Backstroke with confidence, it may be time to show him or her the correct leg movements. Remember, the Elementary Backstroke is a safety/survival stroke, meaning "less is more." The fewer the strokes, the more energy you save. This stroke is recommended when wearing a PFD.

Kicking for the Elementary Backstroke

Beginners will use the flutter kick, and more advanced swimmers will use the inverted frog kick. These are two basic kicks used for four different types of strokes.

The flutter kick can be used with the Elementary Backstroke. It later can be used when the child learns the American Crawl or Freestyle, the Racing Backstroke. The inverted frog kick is the same kick the child will later use in the Breast Stroke, except it is inverted, which means the child performs this kick while swimming on his or her back. The inverted frog kick is better because you have more glide time using this kick. Having more glide allows you to rest between each stroke. That is why the Elementary Backstroke is called the resting stroke. Teach it in the beginning with the flutter kick because it's easier to think about the arm movements without the leg movements. Some people do the frog kick naturally. You will have to find this out about your child as you go along.

Advanced leg movements for the Elementary Backstroke

This stroke looks like an inverted frog kick but it is a little different. It is the more advanced Elementary Backstroke kick. Some of you may be able to do this naturally while you are swimming the Elementary Backstroke. If you know how to do the breast stroke or "frog" kick, doing the Elementary Backstroke kick will be easy because the two are similar. You are on your stomach for the first and on your back for the second.

When done properly, both the Elementary Backstroke kick and the frog kick give the swimmer a lot of kicking power, more so than with any other stroke. These are the only two strokes where the kicking power is comparable to the arm power.

The frog kick is much lower in the water and uses a lot more energy. The Elementary Backstroke kick is much higher in the water. You kick much less frequently and you glide more.

First, your child sits on the side of the pool and you stand in the pool. You show the child the leg movements by moving the child's legs.

1. Hold your child's calves and lift the knees up together about 1/2 way to the child's stomach. The child can have her arms behind her supporting her so she doesn't tip back.
2. Take her feet, turn them about 45 degrees outward.
3. Then pull her legs toward you and separate them about 45°. Then slowly bring her straightened legs together.

Repeat about five times.

Then have the child do the first two steps with your help. At the third step tell your child while she's putting her legs into the 45 degree stretch, the whole motion should speed up into a whipping action. That will give your child the momentum to go forward once she is in the water.

Then you can practice this kick on your stomach in the pool. You can hold your child under the armpits while she is floating backward and practicing the frog kick. This way you can see if the kick is going well.

If it looks good, give your child a kick board and have her practice the frog kick while on her stomach and holding the kick board. The flotation device will hold up the child in the water so she can practice her leg movements without having to think about arm movements. After every kick, have her glide for a second or two and then kick again.

The next step is putting the noodle under her arms, and adding the arm movements for the Breast Stroke kick to the frog kick she's been doing. You can also practice the frog kick holding the wall.

Leg movements; frog kick

You are looking for three separate movements all done one right after the other so it seems like one movement. It should look like a frog kicks, that is why we call it the frog kick. Your child may enjoy your saying, "You're kicking like a frog!"

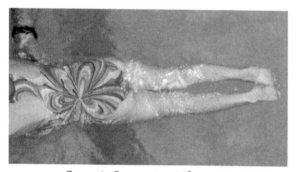
Step 1. Legs straight out.

Step 2. Bend knees and bring feet up.

Step 3. Separate legs and start to bring feet down and back to the first position in a whip-like action.

Step 4. Bring feet and legs back to the original position. Straighten knees and bring feet back together. Repeat.

What the parent says is, "Bend your knees up, turn your feet out, straighten your knees, and pull your feet together fast." Repeat.

This will give you forward momentum. For the Elementary Backstroke, do the same kick, only you are on your back.

For some, this leg action comes naturally. If your child does this naturally, do not try to improve on it.

Putting the arm and leg movements together

Next, try to have the arms and legs work together. Remember for the Elementary Backstroke, we say, "soldier, chicken, T!" In the "soldier" position (in the glide position) your legs are straight and together. At "chicken," bend your knees. When we say "T", turn your feet out together in an extended V-shape, and then you are ready for the power phase of the stroke, the glide. When we say "soldier," extend feet down in a whipping action and bring your legs together and push your arms to the side. Your knees are straightened. When you are finished you should be back in the glide position and your arms will be at your sides. Stay in the glide position until you feel like you've almost stopped gliding. Then start the stroke all over again. Remember: this is a stroke where you try to conserve energy.

Breast Stroke

This skill is best learned by children over four years old. They should be able to stand in the shallow end of the pool. Younger children can also learn this skill if they are wearing a flotation device. Some children do the Breast Stroke naturally. This is worth a try if your child is having a problem with the Doggy Paddle.

The Frog

When teaching this class, first Mike asks the children if they know how to speak Frog. They all look at him with a strange expression. Then Mike tells them that somewhere, one of their great-great-ancestors might have been a frog. The children still have that expression on their faces.

Mike asks them to say, "Ribbit." He points to one of the children and asks the child to say, "Ribbit." The child says, "Ribbit."

Mike says, "You have a frog in your history. And that means you can do the frog kick. But I'm not going to tell you what it is." He goes to the next child and repeats the story. You can do this individually with your child.

Now that your child realizes that he or she can speak Frog, the child might seem pretty impressed. The child may feel confident with the idea that the child can do the frog kick, even though the child does not know what you are talking about.

If you do this with your child, tell him or her that when you got your family coat of arms, there was a little frog on the corner. Be creative and say things like, "This is why our family has such good water skills. At one time we were in the water, and now we're on land."

Mike then asks the child, "Have you ever seen a frog swim? Think of what a frog's legs do." That allows the child to have the idea of what he or she is supposed to do because the frog kick is completely different from the flutter kick.

Then, Mike gives the child a kick board or a flotation device to hold on to, or just holds the child's hands in the water and walks backwards, and he asks the child to do the frog kick.

Some children do this naturally. That's why Mike doesn't demonstrate. First, see if your child can do it. This is better than showing your child, since for this skill, group instruction of the skill is confusing.

If the child can't do the frog kick, then just go to the flutter kick with the same arm movements (described below). That is acceptable.

You've told the frog story. Ask the child to try to do the Breast Stroke by pushing off the wall and swimming to you a few feet away.

We don't worry about learning the frog kick until the child says, "I'm ready to learn it." It's a difficult kick. Unless your child has use of a pool to practice, it's hard to learn. This stroke requires a lot of practice. See the Index for more information about the frog kick.

The Arm Movements

You can start to learn this while standing in the shallow end of the pool. Put your hands together in front of your chest.

When teaching the arm movements for the Breast Stroke, say, "Remember that your hands are always open and flat." When you do the Breast Stroke, first you demonstrate it, then tell your child how to do it.

Put your palms together in front of your chest. Then push them out in front of you all the way. Roll your hands so your palms are facing out. The backs of your hands are now touching. Pull your hands away from each other and back to where your elbows were.

Squeeze your palms together again in front of your chest, where you started.

As you get more proficient in this stroke, the shape of your hand movements becomes less like a circle than an upside-down heart. (This can come when the child is ready. Four years old is too young to expect this.)

Have the child practice the arm movements by walking around the shallow end and doing the motions with you. Repeat, "Cut the pizza in half, make a pizza."

Words of praise: "You're improving every time. Fine job."

When your child can do that pretty well, you can go to the side of the pool and work on the next step.

The way you tell your child is: "Cut a pizza in half." This is the motion from palms together at chest, to palms pushing out.

When you roll the palms over, and pull back to where the elbows are, you say "Make a pizza," because your arm movements form the shape of a pizza, a circle.

She's finished making the pizza. She's bringing her hands back together to repeat the motion.

This is a mom teaching her son how to do the Breast Stroke.

Why not to take your arms out of the water

A good reason for not lifting your arms out of the water is your arms are really buoyant. Even extremely buoyant children who lift their arms out of the water will sink. This will cause a setback. *Have your child keep the arms in the water when you're teaching Elementary Backstroke or Doggy Paddle.* A child needs his or her arms in the water to stay afloat. This is why we learn to blink our eyes instead of rubbing our eyes (see Index). This is also why we do not lift our arms out of the water for the Elementary Backstroke. Even though you swim more slowly, you are sinking less, because you stay at the surface more easily.

Lifting your arms out of the water

This helps your child prepare for the head's-up Crawl. It's also called "Freestyle" swimming or the American Crawl.

The only way to compensate for taking your arms out of the water is to add some speed and forward momentum to your swimming. You must be in a more horizontal position. This causes your body to lift in the water (less drag) and you glide more easily. By lifting your arm out of the water, you create less drag, and create more glide, so you don't have to use as much energy to move forward in the water.

After your child has learned the Doggy Paddle, the next step is learning to lift an arm out of the water while swimming. Instead of saying to the child, "Reach and Dig!" you now say, "Lift your arm, reach and dig." It's good to practice this stroke first on dry land.

When we say "lift" we mean lifting your elbow out of the water until your hand comes out of the water, then putting your hand in front of your head. Then, put your hand back in the water and do the long Doggy Paddle. When the child's head is in the water, and the child is blowing bubbles, this keeps her in a more horizontal position. For this, the child should wear goggles to help her swim in a straight line: she can look down. (Many pools have lines painted on the bottom.)

If your child tries to swim this stroke with her head out of the water, it is much harder to learn. A good way to teach this stroke is to tell the child to take a deep breath and blow bubbles while she does this stroke. Sometimes she can only do two or three strokes, sometimes more. When she runs out of air, she should stop. If she wants to continue to swim, she can do the long Doggy Paddle until she gets air, and then when she's comfortable, she can put her head back in the water and try to swim the Crawl again.

As she gets better at this, she does less long Doggy Paddle and more Crawl.

If your child gets tired, have her go to the stroke she does well, for example, flip over, do the Elementary Backstroke, and rest a while. The best stroke is the one your child goes to when she is tired. When she is rested, suggest she go back to practicing the Crawl. Say: "You're doing great! That's wonderful."

Freestyle or the American Crawl

Children as young as four can sometimes learn this. (We will use the term "Crawl" instead of the technical terms.) The new way to teach the Crawl is teaching it as an extension of the long Doggy Paddle. Show your child how to do this before you ask the child to do it. As your child is doing the Doggy Paddle, she lifts each arm out of the water after each stroke of the Doggy Paddle. This is a simple way to learn and it makes for a more natural stroke.

The Crawl involves lifting your arms out of the water. Often what happens when you lift your arms out of the water is your whole body sinks lower in the water. Teaching the Crawl as an extension of the Doggy Paddle helps prevent that from happening. The child may feel like she's sinking a lot, but often she sinks very little.

The old way to teach the head's up Crawl

As with all lessons, this starts with show and tell. Show your child what to do, and tell her what you are doing as you demonstrate this.

Practice all the strokes on land first, then demonstrate in the pool. You can practice with your child at home before coming to the pool.

This is how we learned it. It's a little more difficult than teaching from the Doggy Paddle, but it still can be used.

Do not stand with your feet together. While out of the water, stand with one foot forward. This makes the rotating motion easier. It's also the position of the legs while the feet are kicking.

Work with one arm at a time. While standing up, not in the pool, put one arm straight in the air, reaching for the ceiling. Your palm is facing forward. Reach far away with your hand straight. Bring your arm down in front of you and touch your leg. Bring your arm up around behind you and back up to where you started.

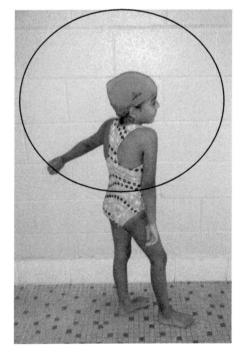

Do this motion five times with each arm. The arm is straight and you're looking straight ahead. When you've got it right with one arm, put that arm down, and try doing this with the other arm.

Your arm is always moving in the direction your palm is facing.

Stand with one shoulder about eight to ten inches from the wall. Put the foot that is furthest from the wall one step ahead. Make believe you are holding a piece of chalk. Then get a sense of the big sweep of the circle by standing by a wall and pretending that the wall is a black board and you are drawing big circles on it. Have your child try pretending this as well.

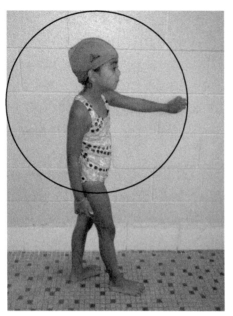

You cannot make the circle without rotating your shoulders. This is a good way to learn how move your arm for the Freestyle (and the racing Backstroke if you do it in reverse). It's very good for rotating your shoulders, a skill you will need for learning how to breathe when doing the Freestyle. You also rotate your shoulders when doing the racing Backstroke.

The child is learning how to rotate her shoulders; that's why she stands close to the wall.

Still out of the water, the next step is to start with one arm straight up in the air and the other arm down by your thigh. At the same time the arm in the air moves down, the hand by the leg moves up.

Remind your child to try to keep elbows straight, the head up, and the head straight. If your child is bending her elbow as she strokes, hold your child's hand to help keep the arm straighter. Children around five or six years old do what they can. They often bend their elbows, and that's fine. By the time they get to age six or seven, they improve. You don't have to worry about "forcing" or "straining" for perfection. Eventually your child will grow into getting this. A lot of children move their heads a lot when they do this. That's fine. Many people, once in the water, practice this with a flotation device.

Words of praise: "Nice moves."

Breathing after lifting the arms—Proper American Crawl

The parent is telling the child to lift her elbow out of the water, blow bubbles, and reach and pull. The parent is giving the child a little support around her stomach so that when she lifts her arms out of the water and loses buoyancy, she will feel supported. Until your child picks up speed, she may sink a little when lifting the arm. If she feels like she's falling, she may panic.

The parent is telling the child to lift the elbow until her hand comes out of the water, and "reach and pull with your other arm. Take your hand and put it in front of your head and then back in the water."

The parent tells the child to turn her head when she lifts her elbow out, and to take a breath. Always one arm is pulling a stroke for power, while the other arm is "recovering" out of the water. When it's out of the water, there's no drag.

After she takes her breath, as her arm crosses her face, she puts her head back in the water, and her arm continues to return to the water. This is fun to practice at home, as slowly as you can. Your child can walk through the house swimming.

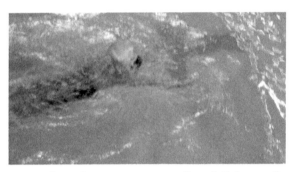

Now that the parent sees the child can do the movement on her own, the parent lets her go. This makes the parent feel like he or she has an Olympic star.

She's lifting her elbow out of the water, starting to rotate her shoulders. It makes breathing a little easier. But, she still has a long way to go. Encourage her. Even though she's swimming, she has a lot of practice ahead. Good swimmers practice frequently.

Her head is turned and she's breathing. Her elbow is high out of the water, and she's breathing in.

Now her arm is returning to the water, and she's also returning her face to the water.

Now she is swimming nicely.

This is for children who are comfortable with the Doggy Paddle. This is not a fun skill, so have your child do it for a short time, not more than five minutes. If your child is getting tired, move on to something else. You want to have fun.

As your child becomes more proficient with breathing, the child can move on to more skillful breathing: instead of lifting her head, the child could turn her head to one side and then put it back into the water.

Demonstrate first. Have your child pick the most comfortable side to tilt her head. A good way to practice this is to have the child hold the side of the pool and practice kicking. While she is kicking, have her exhale with her head in the water and when she needs air, tell her to turn her head to the side to inhale. What makes breathing easier is body rotation. When the child starts to turn her head to breathe, she lifts the elbow out of the water on the side that she's breathing, and the higher she lifts her elbow, the more body rotation. The rest of the head and the other ear should stay in the water. She turns the head enough to let the mouth clear the water. She breathes in rapidly. Then she finishes the stroke, puts her arm back in front of her head and holds the wall. While she does this, the head turns back into the water. Then she starts to blow bubbles slowly. It's two thirds expel air, one third inhale—in terms of time. As the child gets faster it becomes more like three quarters to one quarter.

Some people may not have a gutter on the pool to hold on. You can use an empty orange juice container with the plastic cap screwed on, or a kick board, or you can work with your hands.

In any case, once she works on this at the wall, she's ready to work with her parent's hands in the water. Another way to practice breathing is by using a kick board. Demonstrate this first.

If you're using your hands to support your child (and walking backward), it's easier for her to take a stroke, because you can counter-balance your child's weight with your other hand.

Have your child hold the kick board out in front, like Superman flying. Then have the child kick across the pool, lifting her head when she needs to breathe. The adult puts one hand on the kick board and one hand is supporting her stomach. This helps her get started. A child of four can usually do this after she's learned all the previous skills.

When your child gets more proficient, have her turn her head to breathe instead of lifting her head. If she is using the kick board, it's easier to turn the kick board for rotation than it is to lift her arm and take a stroke. She is leaving her ear in the water. That's good. If your child can't leave her ear in the water, she can turn the kick board instead. Either way is fine. If done together, they are both fine. Any effort your child makes is good, as long as the child is not drinking the pool water. Go easy on your child.

Now she's on her own. She's kicking and blowing bubbles, getting her head ready to pick up to breathe.

She's breathing on the opposite side. Some children are more comfortable breathing on one side than another.

You can also make this a challenge by saying, "Let's see how far you can go. Can you go as far as me?" or "See how many times you can breathe before you get to the other side."

The reason to teach your child to keep her head in the water is it ultimately makes swimming easier. When your head is out of the water, it makes you drop your hips lower. This makes it harder to swim because there's more drag. Your arms will also not have to work as hard if you keep your head in the water. You will have more glide. (See the Index for the exercise holding the side of the pool and blowing bubbles with your head in the water.) Words of praise: "That's right. Beautiful work."

Treading Water

Treading water is an important skill for anybody who wants to swim in the deep end of the pool (where the water is over your head). It's a good skill to have for deep water confidence. Children can learn this in the shallow end, if their feet don't touch the bottom of the pool there. If you're teaching this, you can just walk the child to the depth where he or she can't stand, but you still can stand in the water.

There are two parts to this skill. Leg movements and arm movements. First explain the skills, because you have to do both of them at the same time.

With your legs, you have a choice of motions. For young children, we tell them to "ride a bicycle" in the water or just do a flutter kick: point your toes to the bottom of the pool and kick. Or you can tell the child to run slowly.

The arm movements are a little more "scientific." Your hands are like an airplane wing. Your arms go back and forth (elbow bent) from behind the shoulder to in front of your chest. The motion repeats. The palm is always slightly tilted in the direction it's going. Your arms have to be under the water at all times for buoyancy.

Your head position is important. Your head should be tilted back and your ears should be in the water. The mouth is at the highest point, so you can leave your mouth open and breathe.

If you are going to go into the deep water, you THE ADULT have to have a noodle or a PFD for yourself, for buoyancy. You must be confident in what you're doing, or DO NOT DO IT.

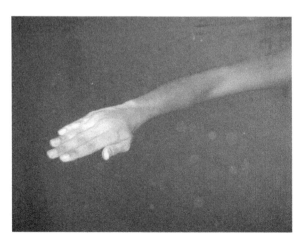

This is what your hand and arm look like when your finning for treading water.

Support your child's head by the back of the neck. You are not holding tight, you are just supporting the child. Tell the child to look toward the ceiling and breathe through her mouth. Tell your child to pretend to ride a bicycle with her legs.

The child may be very scared. Reassure your child that you have them and everything will be OK. Also tell your child that her hands should be flat and open, palms down.

Have the child fin her hands back and forth underwater, like you practiced on deck. Keep breathing through the mouth. When finning, the hands are slightly tilted up (thumbs down) and away from the body when they're going away from the body. That creates lift. They are slightly tilted up (thumbs up) toward the body when coming toward the body. That also creates lift. In this picture the child's hands are coming toward the body. The hand tilting is good, but the fingers should be closed.

As your child starts to relax, start to release your grip but always stay close to catch the child. This builds deep water confidence. Try saying this: "I'm going to count to 10 and then you'll do it all by yourself. I'll be here to catch you if you need me. Open your mouth and breathe and look at the ceiling. Don't move your hands too fast. Try to relax. The more relaxed you are, the more buoyant you are. That means you'll float better."

This is what hands look like while finning and treading water.

This is finning while kicking your feet in the water.

This is finning while pretending to ride a bicycle in the water.

The best way to practice this is: If you have a partner or you're teaching it to your child, you can stand behind her and hold the back of her head and talk her through what she is doing. As she moves her arms and legs and becomes more buoyant, you can move your hand away and let her do it by herself. Be ready to replace your hand if she starts to sink.

If you are trying to learn this on your own, go to the side of the pool up to the point where the water is at the height of your neck. Hold the pool with one hand. Practice bending your knees and doing the motions with one arm at a time. Practice right and left, lifting your feet off the bottom. When you feel comfortable, don't let go of the side, but hold the side of the pool as if you were playing the piano. When you feel comfortable with that, make sure you can still stand in the water (you're not over your head), tilt your head back. Bend your knees. Try treading water.

Low end jumping

This is a good way to practice jumping in but it has to be supervised by an adult. A child wearing floaties should keep fingers interlaced and palms together so the floaties do not come off.

This child says, "I know how to jump in." I say, "OK, let me see." I am in the pool.

She makes a decision mid-air to return to the deck of the pool. This is very common with children who are nervous about jumping in. They might turn around mid-jump and try to grab the edge of the pool. You must know your child. The best way to teach this is to start off holding hands. If you don't, your child risks banging her face on the deck of the pool.

For a nervous child, say, "I'm going to hold your hands this time. We're going to do it together.

The first thing you have to tell her is, "Put your toes over the edge." You can see that she's nervous by the expression on her face and the way she holds her body. She looks like she's going to jump in right to the teacher rather than into the water. Get ready to catch her.

Grip her hands gently (they may disengage in the jump), and tell her she's going to be OK. Say, "We're going to do this together on the count of three. One two three." Notice the teacher is stepping backward to give her room to land in the water and not on the teacher.

When she entered the water, the teacher held her hands lightly and just let her body go into the water. The teacher said, "What a jumper! You're the best." The teacher didn't let her head go underwater, because it might have scared her. Putting your head underwater on your first or second jump can be frightening.

For a child four years old and older, do as follows: Have her stand on the deck. Put her arms out to the side. Have her jump up and down three times and bend her knees when she comes down. Tell her, "That's what it will feel like when you jump in, because your feet will touch the bottom."

Have the child come to the side of the pool. Put her toes over the edge (so the feet don't slip back). Have her bend her knees. Remind your child to jump away from the wall (some children jump out and try to turn around and grab the wall. Remind her that she does not have to turn because you are right there to help.) Say, "OK, jump towards me but don't jump on me." You are standing in the water in case she needs you. If you see anything that you think needs correcting, don't tell the child she did anything wrong. Praise the child first, "Terrific job!" If there are any corrections to be made, say, "This could be a little bit better if you do this..."

Deep end jumping

Unsafe and safe deep-end jumping. If the child on the left loses hold of the noodle when he jumps in, he may panic and drown. If the child on the right loses the noodle, he has a Coast Guard approved PFD on and he will stay at the surface of the water and enjoy the rest of his day. He'll still have fun in the deep end.

He loses the noodle and now what can he do? Unless he has some water safety skills, he will panic.

When children get good at treading water in the shallow end, you can go to the deep end. Say, "Now we're going to have some fun. Let's go to the deep end." Make it exciting.

If you are not comfortable in the deep end, this skill should be taught by someone who is comfortable and skilled, or by a water safety instructor.

First talk through and then demonstrate what you want your child to learn. Your child should stand beside the pool and watch you. Say what you do as you do these things.

"Watch: my toes are over the edge. I bend my knees, take a deep breath, put my arms out to the sides, and I jump straight out. I don't jump near the wall. Three-two-one-go." Jump in. When you come up, say, "In the water I kick up. I move my arms. Notice that I don't rub my eyes. I blink to keep the water out. If I pull my hands out of the water, I sink more easily." Demonstrate this.

Demonstrate kicking up to the surface several times.

"I'm underwater for about three seconds, one-two-three. Then I come up to the surface. I put my head back and I take a breath of air. When I come to the surface, I tread water a few seconds."

"You don't have to move really fast. If you move nice and slow, your natural buoyancy will help keep you afloat."

"Do you want to try? Be sure not to jump on me." You're in the water now, a few feet away from the wall.

The child will use the same movements he used in the low end to tread water. Tell him to do the Elementary Backstroke to get to the surface of the water. The child comes up within three seconds. If he doesn't, reach down and bring him up to the surface.

If the child takes a deep breath before jumping in, his lungs will be full of air and he should rise to the surface. When he comes to the surface, say, "You're OK, you're on the surface. Tilt your head back. Look at up at the ceiling (or the sky)." Support the back of the child's head until you know he's treading water on his own. "Take a deep breath. Breathe through your mouth. Move your arms back and forth with your palms down. You're fine. You're doing great."

Continue supporting the back of the child's head.

Take his head, and have the top of the child's head touch your chest. Tell him, "I'm going to let you go, and you'll do it on your own for ten seconds. And we'll count." Count to ten with your child, constantly giving positive feedback, "Terrific." If the child is not doing great, place your hand underneath the back of the child's head to support him. Take a look at how he is treading water. Make sure his palms are facing the right way. Make sure he is kicking his legs.

If the child is doing well, move away, and try a three second count.

If it works, and he is staying afloat, tell him, "You're doing great. Now we're going to stop and swim to the side of the pool." Then you can repeat the exercise.

If a child is very tense, he's not as buoyant. With practice, he'll be more relaxed.

Once your child is doing this with confidence, you can go back to counting to ten. After that, he can start jumping in the deep end and swimming toward the shallow end WITH SUPERVISION.

Children always have more confidence when they know they're swimming toward the low end than when they know they're swimming toward the deep end.

Some kids will not jump. You may have to go back to the shallow end, and move the child slowly toward the deep end. If your child is very afraid of jumping in the deep end, have him sit on the wall and just fall in, and catch his hands when he comes in. Don't catch his whole body. Turn him around toward the ladder and let him get out. Slowly have him work his way in. Don't push. Save treading water until he is comfortable jumping in.

You can always ask the lifeguard to watch the practice. This way you have an extra eye on the whole thing.

Words of praise: "Exactly right! You make my job fun."

Deep-end jumping can still be a lot of fun, as you can see here. However, be sure to supervise this so that children wait in line and do not jump on each other. We advise NO DIVING. Even though this pool is a private pool with a small diving board, you can dive off this board and hit the bottom. (See pages 22-23 for creative jumping ideas.) NO DIVING.

Songs and Fun

Songs are a wonderful teaching tool. They're useful as a break between lessons. And they're fun.

If you are not familiar with any of these songs, you can find them on the Internet and listen to them.

If you're happy and you know it, blow some bubbles.
Sung to the tune of, *"If you're happy and you know it clap your hands."*

Demonstrate for your child before you start: "When I say kick your feet, I want to see you kick your feet. Kick your feet underwater, no splashing. Sing with me. I want to hear it."

If you're happy and you know it, blow some bubbles
If you're happy and you know it, blow some bubbles
If you're happy and you know it, and you really want to show it,
If you're happy and you know it, blow some bubbles.

If you're happy and you know it, paddle your arms
If you're happy and you know it, paddle your arms
If you're happy and you know it, and you really want to show it,
If you're happy and you know it, paddle your arms.

If you're happy and you know it, kick your feet
If you're happy and you know it, kick your feet
If you're happy and you know it, and you really want to show it,
If you're happy and you know it, kick your feet.

Baby Beluga by Raffi
This is a wonderful swimming song, which you can find on the Internet. The chorus goes, *"Baby Beluga in the deep blue sea, swims so wild and swims so free."* Children just love it.

If anyone in the pool has a birthday, you can sing *Happy Birthday* in the pool. And you can paddle your arms to the tune of *Happy Birthday*. Again, this is a song you can find easily on the internet.

Swim in the Pool

This is sung to the tune of *Row, row, row your boat.*

Swim swim swim in the pool
gently in the pool
merrily merrily merrily merrily
the pool is full of fun

Paddle, paddle, paddle your arms
gently in the pool
merrily merrily merrily merrily
the pool is full of fun.

Kick kick kick your feet
gently in the pool
merrily merrily merrily merrily
the pool is full of fun.

Blow blow blow your bubbles
gently in the pool
merrily merrily merrily merrily
the pool is full of fun.

When I'm in the Water I Blow Some Bubbles!

(This is sung to the tune of *The Wheels on the Bus*, which you can find on the Internet.)

Start out by singing **The Wheels on the Bus**.

When I'm in the water I blow some bubbles,
Blow some bubbles, blow some bubbles.
When I'm in the water I blow some bubbles all day long!

When I'm in the water I paddle my arms,
Paddle my arms, paddle my arms!
When I'm in the water I paddle my arms all day long.

When I'm in the water I kick my feet,
Kick my feet, kick my feet.
When I'm in the water I kick my feet all day long.

When I'm in the water I float on my back,
Float on my back, float on my back.
When I'm in the water I float on my back all day long!

Here's another version of a song sung to the tune of **The Wheels on the Bus**. We use it when we are teaching about following rules. The words get sort of jammed in, which makes it kind of funny for the kids.

"When I'm in the pool I follow the rules, follow the rules, follow the rules" [you can point to the rules on the wall while you sing]... When I'm in the pool I follow the rules, all day long..."

"When I'm in the pool, I swim with a partner, swim with partner, swim with a partner" [point to your partner] "When I'm in the pool I swim with a partner. I never swim without one....."

"When I'm in the pool I look for a lifeguard" [put your hand on your forehead like a visor and look for the lifeguard] "look for a lifeguard, look for a lifeguard. When I'm in the pool I look for a lifeguard, I never swim without one......"

"When I'm in the pool, I'm having lots of fun [wiggle your hands in the air], having lots of fun, having lots of lots fun. When I'm in the pool we're having lots of fun, because I'm staying safe. Yippeee!"

A Few Fun Games
Ping-Pong Ball Race

Bring a couple of ping-pong balls. In the shallow end, using your breath, blow a ping-pong ball across the surface of the water. Swim from one side of the pool to the other. Try not to touch the ball with your hands. Try to do this without your feet touching the the bottom of the pool. You and your child can race, or your child can race other children who are also blowing ping-pong balls. It's fun to bring in other people to cheer from the sidelines. Words of praise: "That's right! Fantastic."

Games to play using properly fitting goggles or opening your eyes underwater.

Children four years old and up can enjoy this after they learn bubble-blowing skills. Opening your eyes underwater can be the most challenging experience for a newcomer. Opening your eyes under the water can sting. Your vision is blurry. It's a different experience.

Some teaching tools which may be helpful:

1. Have the child go under a limbo stick in the water.

2. Have the child try to go through a submerged hula hoop without touching it.

3. If you have other participants, play Ring Around the Rosy in the pool. Hold hands and sing, "Ring around the rosy, pocket full of posy. Ashes, ashes we all fall down." And dunk in the water.

4. For the more advanced child or adult: Try going under the water's surface to touch the pool floor with your hand or try to pick up an object from the pool floor.

The following things are not covered by this book:

• The Deep Water Huddle
• Recovering objects in deep water
• Rotary Breathing
• Somersaults in the water
• Back Stroke
• Butterfly Stroke
• Diving

To learn these skills, we suggest you take Red Cross certified swim instruction.

~~ SPLASH ~~

PART III: Safety
What parents need to know to keep children safe

Read this section thoroughly. Your child's life may depend on it.
Drowning can happen in seconds.

We take safety very seriously, because if you're really careful about safety, you can confidently go into the water with your child and have the best kind of fun.

Even a child who has taken a course or is a confident swimmer may not be safe. Drowning is one of the leading causes of accidental death among children. More than half the people who drown never intended to get wet. The main cause of drowning is panic: older children panic because they don't have skills (if a child is really young, the child won't panic, he or she will just go under.) After that, the next leading cause of accidental death is hypothermia.

The safest child is an informed (but not terrified) child. A child with more water safety information and skills is safer than a child who doesn't have that information and those skills. It's not how well you swim that matters, it's how much you know about water safety. Even the best swimmers in the world can drown.

Always supervise your child in or near a body of water.

Constant vigilance is probably the best approach for parents, but even with the best of intentions, it's easy for you to get distracted. Children can fall into a pool so quietly. **There is no such thing as "drown proofing" a child or a body of water. If you're worried about your child, put a Coast Guard approved life preserver (also known as a PFD or personal flotation device) on her or him.**

If you buy a PFD for a child, you can use it whenever the child needs one. We believe PFD ownership should be mandatory, like car safety seats. (See the Index for more information on PFDs.)

Set a good example: Behave in a safe way.
Children mimic what you do. If you act safe, they'll act safe. You can have a lot of fun and still obey the rules and be safe. You have to show them that.

Sometimes you have to be creative to do that. It may seem like fun to jump off the garage roof into the pool, but it's dangerous. (See the section on jumping in the pool for more information.)

Drinking alcohol and going in the water don't mix. **Swim sober.** Often, around pools, adults are drinking alcohol. Boating events also often have a lot of drinking. Half of the swimming and boating accidents are alcohol-related. Never supervise your child around water of any kind if you have taken drugs or alcohol.

A Puddle Jumper (we don't know why it's called that) in use as a flotation device. The "puddle jumper" is a relatively new Coast Guard-approved #3 jacket that is good for children weighing between 30 and 50 pounds. Children find it much more comfortable than traditional PFDs.

Back of puddle jumper. This is how the puddle jumper is attached in the back, so the child cannot take it off, and it cannot come off when they jump in. See the Index for information on flotation devices.

Rules for Safety

These are rules, not suggestions, that you and your children should follow. The younger that children learn the rules, the safer they are. Please follow these rules yourself as well.

You have to take precautions your child would never think of. Children often act without thinking. Your child wants to just jump in and have fun. Every time you go to a swim facility, you have to explain to your child what's going on.

For example, you can run on a beach because you have sure footing in the sand. However, you walk at pools and water parks because it is very easy to slip. Basically, people who follow the rules get to have a good time and they usually go home without unfortunate incidents.

Before you leave your house, always take a minute to talk about safety. Before the child gets excited about being in the water, while the child is still calm and listening, explain the rules.

Here are some of the basic rules:

1. **You are responsible for your child's safety.** Lifeguards and PFDs help, but the safety job is yours.

2. **Walk. Don't run**. Most injuries caused by running can be prevented by slowing the child down. This also means having kids stay away from rough physical play.

Whenever possible, have the child wear pool shoes, with traction on the soles, when you're by the pool. We've seen many accidents because people run or don't watch their footing.

3. **Only go in the water with parental supervision.** When no one is watching your child, your child is in danger of drowning. If your child is a non-swimmer, he or she should wear a PFD unless you are in the water with the child.

4. **Obey all the rules of a swimming facility**. Usually rules are posted. Make it a policy whenever you go to a new facility to find out where rules are posted and to read the rules out loud with your child. Reward your child for knowing safety features. For example, these are some rules that we have seen:

   - No swimming without a lifeguard present.
   - Everyone must shower before entering the pool.
   - No running, pushing or diving in shallow water.
   - No hanging on the ropes.
   - No going in the pool while chewing gum or wearing bandages.
   - Everyone must wear a bathing cap.
   - No smoking.
   - No back diving.
   - No soda, glass bottles, or food in the pool area.
   - The swimming session ends fifteen minutes before closing of buildings.
   - No swimming in the diving area.
   - No spitting.

Rules change at different types of swimming facilities, such as water parks, lakes, oceans and pools, so check them out each time.

You can introduce the rules with songs when the child is up to five years old (see pages 136-8 for swimming songs.)

With children over four years old, you can introduce the rules with sayings, such as "Look before you leap!" **You, the parent, have to judge when the child is ready to understand these basic rules.** Mike is a Red Cross certified instructor, and this is how he was trained to introduce the rules (with thanks to the Red Cross):

   - "Swim with a buddy in a supervised area."
   - "Be Cool, Follow the Rules."
   - "Think so you don't sink."
   - "Reach or throw ... Don't go."
   - "Don't just pack it, wear your jacket." [We mean your PFD]
   - "Cold can kill." (For more information on hypothermia, see the Index).

Basic swimming rules. These are rules that you may not see posted:

- Swim only at places with a lifeguard.
- If you're very tired, very cold, or overheated, stay out of the water.
- Obey the lifeguard's instructions
- If you can't see the bottom of the pool in the deep end or if the water is cloudy, swim someplace else.
- At night, only swim in a well-lit place.
- Food is for dry land. Do not eat while swimming. You could choke.
- Horseplay is dangerous. Do not push, shove, or run near the water.
- If you hear thunder or see lightning, get out of the water.
- Swim a safe distance away from diving boards and slides—never under them.

If your child has to go to the bathroom, take your child there. It's essential that your child knows it's not good to pee in the water. The words, "Don't pee in the pool" are crucial. Say to your child, "Tell me if you need to pee."

Safety Tips for Different Types of Swimming Facilities

Every place you go to use water for recreation has unique qualities and potential hazards. When you know the dangers, you may be able to prevent trouble from occurring.

Once you get to a swim area...

If you're new at a place, and you don't see rules, with your child in tow, go to the lifeguard or someone in charge and say, "We're new. Do you have any special rules?" The answers might surprise you. Some places don't want kids swimming under the lifeguard chair. Some insist you wear a cap. Some pools clear the water of swimmers every hour or so for the adults to have a few minutes to swim.

Let the lifeguard know your child's abilities; for example, whether your child is a swimmer or a non-swimmer. "We've got an adorable little non-swimmer here!"

If the rules are posted, again, read them aloud with your child and talk about what they mean.

As a parent, it's your job to look around to see if there's a safety pole to use to reach into the water to rescue a drowning person. Look for emergency floats. Check the water temperature. Check the depth of the water.

Show your child the deep and shallow ends of the pool. Point out the safety rope, the rope that divides the low end from the deep end. It's also called the "lifeline" because it's in the shallow end to keep you alive if you're a non-swimmer. This rope could be placed in water over the child's head. Find out from the lifeguard how deep the water is at the rope. Let your child know that this rope, for example, is in five feet of water and the child is only three feet high. Tell your child the pool gradually gets deeper. Remember to point out any unsafe conditions to your children. Point out the children who are not obeying the rules, and tell your child to keep away from them. Those children may get hurt or hurt someone else.

Every place you use water for recreation has different qualities and dangers. Learn the risks so you can prevent accidents.

Floating Readiness Skills: Kiddie Pools.

You do not teach children to swim in a kiddie pool. This is a good place to practice floating readiness skills. Kiddie pools vary in depth. As with all pools, your child must be supervised at a kiddie pool. Children have more confidence when they know water is shallow. If you are at a facility with a kiddie pool (usually about eighteen inches deep), allowing your children who can already walk to float while walking on their hands is a good beginning for learning how to float. Then the child can try it with her face in the water. You can also ask the child to do it with one hand touching the bottom, or no hands touching the bottom. You can ask your child to try it on her back with no hands.

If you have a kiddie pool in your yard, empty it after every time you use it. Otherwise, you risk your child going into the back yard and drowning. **Kiddie pools have to be emptied of water after each use.**

Pools. Pools are a good place to teach your child to swim because the water is filtered and chlorinated water is clear, so you can see the child when underwater. Pools fall into two categories: private and public.

Backyard pools. A backyard pool can be a good place to teach your child to swim. However, it is the most dangerous place for an unsupervised child. For your own peace of mind, have a fence and a gate that locks to keep children out. Also use appropriate precautions with spas (Jacuzzis). Jacuzzis should be covered when not in use. In-ground pools can also have a stretch cover that can prevent drowning.

A note about above-ground pools

Horsing around is dangerous in an above-ground pool because you can fall and bang your head on the side of the pool. You should never dive off the side of an above-ground pool. You should never sit your child on the edge of a pool and leave him or her unattended. Sitting on the edge of an above-ground pool is dangerous. Falling backward is a very common accident. Leave the ladder up when the pool is not in use. Even though there is a sign on the ladder saying not to dive, people dive anyway. The largest number of injuries in pools are back and neck injuries from diving in.

Rules for any and all pool slides:

- Go down feet first.
- Sit as you slide.
- Don't do dangerous stunts.

More on public pools. In some states, a public pool does not have to have a lifeguard. These pools will have signs that say, "Swim at your own risk." Also, privately owned community pools at hotels, condominiums, clubhouses or private community centers sometimes do not have to have lifeguards. Supervision is the key to safety. **A LIFEGUARD DOES NOT MEAN YOUR CHILD IS DROWN-PROOFED.** With or without a lifeguard, **YOU must supervise your kids.**

Water Parks. Though water parks are not a great place for teaching your child how to swim, water parks can be fun because they offer something for every age group.

Each attraction may have a different water depth: find and point out the water depth with your child each time you try something new. Before using an attraction, make sure there is a lifeguard for that area. Some facilities provide free PFDs for non-swimmers. Water parks can be busy and crowded. So, make sure your child is wearing a Coast Guard approved PFD at all times. In a wave pool, show your child how to find out the water depth before the waves come. Teach your child to watch for floating objects, and to watch for the signal when the waves start. Some attractions will have a sign with a height level, like a ride in an amusement park. Keep your child at the correct level for his or her size. **Do not make your child go above his or her level.** Make sure your child can stand in the water or that it's shallow enough for him or her to recover and stand. That way, if they slip, they can recover. They might get scared, but they won't get traumatized.

Lakes, ponds, rivers, oceans and other bodies of water require more advanced techniques than this book can cover.

This is a small-town pool. It has a nice feature: a staircase that allows you to enter and exit the pool much more easily.

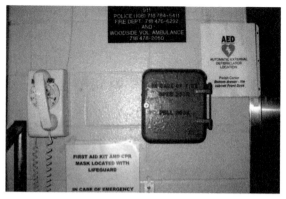

When you enter the pool area, look around for the safety signs and flotation devices that can be used in an emergency.

This is a lifeguard's chair at a public pool. If you're at a pool that has lifeguards, look to see where they stay, and the safety equipment should be around them.

Unsafe toys: This is an unsafe toy because your child can turn upside down. Because it's buoyant, it gives parents a false feeling of safety.

Unsafe toys: The child on the flotation device believes he's rowing a boat and he's safe. He's now in the deep end. The adults are holding on to the side of the pool for support. All he has to do is lose his balance and he's in the water without a PFD, and in trouble.

The wind can blow all the toys to the deep end. Children try to jump into them. Toys move. Children go to the bottom of the pool.

Swim at your own risk. This pool is unsafe because (even though there is a painted line) there is no rope separating the shallow end and the deep end. The shallow part ends abruptly and children playing near there could slip into the deep water and drown.

Unsafe places: parents should watch for places in aquatic areas where even the lifeguard cannot see your child.

Unsafe places: The child may swim out while you are making your dive and you could land on the child. You can't see the child and the child can't see you.

Many children who drown reach for something (toys or a ball)
in the water and fall in.

His toy got away from him.

"What am I going to do?"

"It's coming closer. I'll try to reach for it."

When he tries to reach for it, his body pushes the water which pushes the toy away. He loses the grip on the rail.

Now he has stepped off the steps and is not tall enough to stand. He can drown in twenty to sixty seconds.

No running on deck!

You're going to fall and get hurt!

Don't rely on anyone but yourself for your child's safety. Notice what's missing here. There's no safety rope dividing the deep and the shallow end. A line on the bottom of the pool is not enough. When you go to the pool, if you don't have a cell phone, look for a phone near the pool. If you have a cell phone, make sure you have service before you settle in.

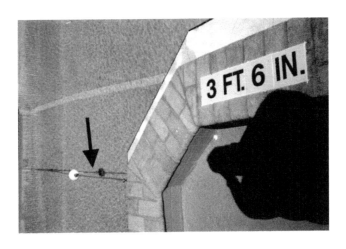

3 FT. 6 IN.

Good fence and a good gate: The gate can make a fence good or bad. A gate that opens easily for children is bad. This gate is 4 feet high and parents have to lift at least 4½ feet to open it. The fence is good because it is four feet high. The outside of the fence has a wind protector. This also makes it difficult for children to climb the fence because they can't get a toe grab.

This is a bad gate. It opens from the outside with a pull-down latch that is only 3 feet high. Even though the fence is 4 feet high all around, a two-foot-tall child could reach up and open the gate.

Close-up of "bad gate" lock.

I've got a good idea!

This ought to do it.

I watched those grown-ups.
I know how to open that lock.

Uh-oh, I can't open
the fence. I have to go
to the other side.

This is a very good lock, but not good enough. It does have a key to lock it but they did not lock it this time. You can use two or three wire ties to shut it, and when you want to open it, cut the wire ties off. You can find them at any hardware store. This pool owner ties his gate every evening.

Now I've got it!

Here I come.

I'm in!

Hurray!
Note to parents:
Without a PFD, this is a tragedy.

We recommend that no child goes in a hot tub. Tubs are as dangerous as pools. Children can fall in. They can get hyperthermia (get too hot). If they have very long hair, it can get stuck in the drain of a Jacuzzi. So, be sure to supervise your child.

The pool is dark. You can't see the bottom. There's not a single safety sign indicating the depth of the water. There's nothing to indicate the temperature of the water. The water was 58 degrees. The optimum temperature for a pool is 86 degrees. If a child or an adult swam in this pool, hypothermia could set in fast. See the Index for more information about hypothermia and hyperthermia.

Private pools, safety and responsibility: This pool has no safety equipment. No rules are posted. Parents: This is your responsibility. The depth is unmarked. The pool was 12 feet at the deep end.

POOL SIGNS

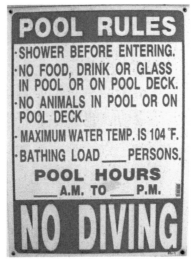

General rules. Rules will change at every pool, so always read the rules.

When a sign says NO SWIMMING, don't swim. Reasons could be anything from bacteria to marine life to unsafe water conditions, to just what's mentioned on this sign.

NO DIVING
Unless you are trained to dive, do not dive. If you are trained, only dive in a diving pool.

The rules, the ring buoy, and the safety hook. The shepherd's hook is hidden behind a plant. It's also bent. It should be U-shaped. The rules are fine.

This rope looks fine from a distance, but look up close.
You might be able to throw the buoy, but you couldn't pull a person back if you wanted to.

~~ SPLASH ~~

Never throw your children high up in the air. They are slippery and you could drop them. A lot of accidents happen this way.

Horsing around on deck is dangerous. Many accidents around pools involve slipping and falling. It could lead to real problems. If she falls in the water, she could hurt herself and others.

She's falling in the water. Someone else could be underneath. There are numerous ways she and others could be hurt here.

Dunking is a bad idea, but children clown around. If your child is wearing a PFD, he will come back to the surface after the dunker stops pushing down. If you see this happening, stop it immediately.

He's pushing him under.

There's a kid like this in all neighborhoods.

Now he's running away: fear of retaliation.

"But I'm OK. I have my PFD on. I pushed away and held my breath."

General Rules about Jumping

Diving is an advanced skill and should be taught by a water safety instructor or a diving coach. Do not teach your child or yourself to dive. Talk with your child about the dangers of diving.

Dangers of Diving In

Both Mike and Andrea know people who have spinal cord injuries from diving. Some have been paralyzed for life, and some have been killed. According to the Spinal Cord Injury Information Network, more than 850 spinal cord injuries result from diving each year. Three hundred of these happened at backyard pools. In 75% of these cases, the pools had no depth indicators. More than 9 out of 10 happened to guests not pool owners. Half occurred during a party.

Diving should only be taught by a professional diving teacher. Do not attempt to teach yourself or teach your child.

If you see your child trying to dive, tell the child to stop. Get the child's attention, and tell him or her it's as dangerous as running in the street without looking. When swimming skills improve, the child can be taught by a water safety instructor or a diving coach in the proper aquatic setting.

We believe diving is only safe under the supervision of a professional diving instructor in a professional diving pool, which is a pool designed solely for diving.

If you have any questions about the safety of your local pool, please consult your local Red Cross or a certified aquatic expert.

Safe Jumping

Always put your toes over the edge before you jump in so you don't slip.

Unsafe Jumping

This is a typically foolish teenager. Most back and neck injuries occur because of shenanigans like this.

Never jump in the pool backwards. You may jump on somebody. You may hurt yourself. You can't put your toes over the edge to prevent slipping. You could slip and bang your own legs while going in. You can't put your hands in front of you to protect yourself.

Never dive at a beach into a wave (or into cloudy murky water)

If you see other people diving, this still does not mean it's safe, especially in unfamiliar places.

Remember the saying, "Look before you leap." (That goes for jumping in, too.) BE CAREFUL. Learn to swim before learning to dive.

Let your child know: even when they know how to swim, diving is dangerous.

There are no exceptions to these suggestions.

Private Open Water Swimming

Only swim in open water with someone who is capable of rescuing you and aware they are watching you. Open water is dangerous. Hypothermia, your body getting too cold, is the second leading cause of drowning. Many excellent swimmers die of hypothermia.

Public open water swimming. This is Michael, the co-author, swimming the open water swim down the Hudson River organized by the Little Red Light House, one of many similar events organizations sponsor throughout the year .

Have an emergency action plan

You know how to leave your home during a fire. You should know what to do in a water emergency. Minutes save lives. Having an **Emergency Action Plan** means having a plan in case there's a problem. Know where the phone is so you can dial 911 for emergency help. Again, make sure your phone has service. Keep a first-aid kit handy. Knowing what to do in an emergency will keep you from panicking and may save a life—your child's or your own. That little bit of confidence gives you the few moments you need to save a life. You will not panic if you've been trained to know what to do. If you don't have to depend on a telephone operator to save a life, that's a wonderful thing. That saves time. Someone else could call for help while you're doing CPR (Cardiopulmonary Resuscitation).

Part of your emergency action plan involves preparing. PLEASE take a course in CPR. That will also teach you how to do the Heimlich Maneuver and how to clear a choking child's throat. Know where the lifeguard is. Know where a working phone is. Know where the nearest hospital is.

This is what we call a distressed swimmer. He's yelling for help.

You can go from being distressed to drowning in seconds.

Active drowning: This is what a drowning child looks like. This child cannot yell for help because he's trying to get air. He can't wave for help because he's trying to use his arms to keep above water. He can't see help because he's looking at the sky trying to keep his mouth up. He's also only a few feet from other swimmers, but they don't realize he's drowning. He will be on the surface of the water less than 60 seconds, and is almost silent. When someone is drowning, they can't make noise. All they are doing is trying to get air.

This is what drowning looks like under the water. He was only inches from the wall.

Dry Drowning

A child has small lungs. If a child gets a small amount of water in the lungs, it can be very dangerous. According to the Centers for Disease Control, 10–15 percent of drownings can be classified as "Dry Drowning." This can occur up to 24 hours after a small amount of water gets in the lungs. This can even happen during a bath.

Three important signs to look for are "difficulty breathing, extreme tiredness and changes in behavior. All are the result of reduced oxygen flow to the brain." Ask your child how he or she feels after a swim if you were not with the child. If you are with your child you will notice the signs. (See www.msnbc.msn.com/id/24982210/ for more about this data.) If these symptoms persist, go straight to the emergency room. This could be a real emergency.

Saving others: What to do if a person is drowning or needs help.

The following is general information about saving others. The first thing you do is start yelling for help. Keep yelling the whole time you're doing these things. If you are not trained in lifesaving procedures, only enter the water if you continue to hold the side of the pool with one hand and reach for the victim with the other, or reach with your foot. The reason is that you could also become a victim and drown. If you can't swim, do not go in the water after a drowning victim. A lot of people drown trying to save somebody else or even trying to save their dogs. Here's what you can do to save someone. This is the proper procedure:

Emergency Skills

Emergency skills can be used by people without lifesaving training to assist someone who is drowning. From the Boy Scouts, we borrow the saying, "Reach, Throw, Go for help." This saying can help you remember what to do when a situation arises. If the person is close enough, do a "reaching assist." If not, throw something buoyant to him or her. If that doesn't work, go for help. If there are two people present, one can "reach, throw…" and the other can go for help. You can also teach this to children. As early as four or five years old, a child can go for help or can throw lifesaving devices in the water.

1. **Reach:** Try to reach the victim with your hand. Make sure that you have a good grasp of something on land or the side of the pool before you reach for the victim. You don't want to fall in or lose your grip. Most pools have a long aluminum pole you can use. Sometimes it has a hook on the end. They're called shepherd's hooks. Even a private pool should have a long pole (with a net on the end) that's used to skim the water. Use the pole to reach the victim if you can't reach by hand. If the person is pulling so hard that they're going to pull you into the water, release the pole or rope or whatever you're holding on to that's pulling you in. Never wrap something around you to hold onto it. It could be used to pull you in. You do not want to be the second victim.

If you want more information about this, read the Red Cross booklet, "Water Safety Handbook."

If you can't reach the person with your hand, you may enter the water as long as you can **hold on with both your hands to the side of the pool (the gutter) or the railing so you have a firm grip**. Then extend your foot to the victim.

This is a reach from the deck to save someone in trouble. Notice how she's holding on the bar so she does not get pulled in.

The person in trouble is a little further out and harder to reach. You may enter the water as long as you can grab something with your hand firmly and extend your foot. Yell to the person, "Grab my foot! Grab my foot!"

2. **Throw.** Throw a floating object to the drowning victim when he or she is too far out to reach. Look around the pool area for a ring buoy, a throw bag, or a rescue tube. As you are doing the rescue, make sure you are loudly yelling "Help!" You want to throw an object with a line attached so the victim can grab it and you can pull him or her to safety. When throwing the floating object to the victim, make sure you have a good grip on the line. Also, remember the drowning victim may not be able to see the rescue buoy. Therefore, try to throw it under his/her arms or past his/her head so you can pull it back towards the person. In an emergency situation, you can throw anything that floats in the water. Use lawn chairs, coolers, swim noodles, or anything else that the victim can grab on to and stay afloat. Try not to hit the victim in the head. Even things you don't think will float might float, so throw everything in.

3. **Go in the water only for a reaching assist, meaning you can reach the victim with your arm or leg while holding on to the side of the pool.** If you are wearing a PFD, you can enter the water to chest height and attempt to reach the person. Take a buoyant object to give to the victim. If you see a rescue situation, and you are not alone, send someone else for help. Call 911. If you can't find a phone and you see a fire box, pull the fire alarm. (Firemen are trained as first responders.)

If you are by yourself, yell for help while you are making the rescue. Do not be afraid of yelling for help. If the person is near the side of the pool, try to make a reaching assist before you go for help.

Grandma took granddaughter to the pool. Granddaughter told Grandma, "I can swim," and jumped in the deep end. She could not swim. Grandma did not panic. She got a lifeguard buoy, tossed it to her granddaughter and held the rope on the other end, and pulled her granddaughter to safety. Grandma says, "I'll teach you how to swim."

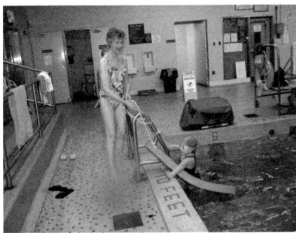

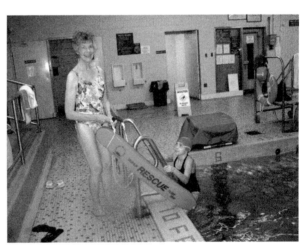

What to tell your kids about safety moves for themselves. Children can learn basic safety information for themselves in the water when they are ready. Children are so different from one another. You are the only qualified judge to decide when your child is ready. The child has to be mature enough to understand about safety. If the child knows about how dangerous it is to cross a street, about waiting for a green light, about the dangers of a hot stove, if your child carries keys, then probably he or she is ready to learn safety around water. Your child must have some respect for the water. This is shown in several ways, such as making sure his or her toes are over the edge of the pool before they jump in; learning something and practicing it; recognizing objects at the pool like the rescue buoy, the lifeguard's chair, the shepherd's hook; asking parents' permission before going in; and recognizing the lifeguard.

Keep reading. It's worth the hour to read all the way through the safety pages. This hour could change your life if you save a life as a result.

Icy water is dangerous water. It is beyond the scope of this book to help you if you get in trouble with this. Keep away from icy water.

If you see your child getting cold,
take him out of the water and warm him up.

Danger signs of Hypothermia. NOTE: If you are in an emergency, call 911.

Your ability to recognize when your child is cold is important. An infant or toddler cannot tell you if he or she is cold. Usually by the time an older child tells you, the child is at the beginning of hypothermia. For infants and toddlers, look for these signs:

- If your child is shivering,
- If your child's lips are turning blue,
- If your child gets a glazed stare, or
- If your child gets listless and apathetic (doesn't care)

   ...then it's time to take her or him out of the pool.

Wrap the child in a warm towel so the evaporating water does not make the child colder, or put the child in a warm shower.

Even if the pool is a good temperature (86° F), half an hour in the pool is enough.

Adults or older children can also become colder in the water. Their judgment is impaired. And eventually they can lose consciousness in the later stages of hypothermia. Hypothermia is a progressive, deadly condition.

The Danger of Getting too Cold (Hypothermia) and What to Do About It

How it works: If you get too cold, it can harm or kill you. Hypothermia is the second leading cause of water-related death (panic is first). Hypothermia occurs rapidly in water: Your body loses heat twenty times faster in cold water than in cold air.

At the early stage, muscles get rigid and thinking gets cloudy. The person may seem confused. The next step is amnesia. When body temperature drops, people don't respond when others speak and then they lose consciousness. At the end stage, you go into cardiac arrest and die. It can set in less than twenty minutes depending on the water temperature and your child's amount of padding and endurance. It happens much faster with young children.

Again, hypothermia is serious. **Get your child to a hospital if you suspect your child has hypothermia.**

WHEN TO ABSOLUTELY GET OUT OF COLD WATER, OR STAY OUT OF THE WATER

1. If your child enters water and starts to **breathe fast** (hyperventilate), the water is too cold. Get the child out. Warm the child up. Change her or him to dry clothes as soon as possible.

2. Do not drink alcohol around aquatic areas. It tricks you. Alcohol does not really make you warmer. Stay sober around kids.

There's a difference between kids whining about cold and cold being a real problem. A cold child stands holding his or her arms and legs close. When a child is warm, the posture is usually relaxed.

Heat-Related Emergencies; If you are in an emergency, call 911.

Heat-related incidents can be dangerous if you don't attend to them promptly. This is especially true for infants and the elderly. Remember, a child is your responsibility and may not know when he or she is too hot. When it's hot out, it is good to spend short amounts of time in the heat, and then rest indoors or in the shade, and cool off. If you see your child is ready to go out again, he or she can go out for more fun.

Signs of heat cramps

If your child has painful muscle spasms, especially in the abdomen and legs, this may be a sign of heat cramps.

What to do:

- Rest your child in a cool place.
- Give your child cool water to drink.
- Gently stretch and massage the muscles.
- Get medical help if the situation does not improve, or if your child vomits or loses consciousness.

Signs of heat illness

If your child is sweating heavily, has "cool, moist, pale or flushed skin," "headache, nausea, or dizziness," and feels exhausted or weak, he or she may be suffering from the early stages of heat illness. The late stages of heat illness are characterized by "red, hot, dry skin," "changes in the level of consciousness," and "vomiting."

What to do:

- Care for your child by moving him or her to a cool place and loosening or removing sweat-soaked clothing. Place wet, cool cloths on your child's skin or mist the child with cool water and fan him or her. If the child is conscious, give her or him cool water to drink.
- If your child "refuses water, vomits, or loses consciousness," phone 911, or send someone to phone. Place your child on his or her side. This way, if you have to leave the child alone and go for help, if the child vomits, he or she won't choke.
- Keep cooling the child by placing cold packs or ice packs on wrists, ankles, groin, neck, and/or armpits.
- Provide rescue breathing and CPR if needed.

(This information comes from the *Red Cross Water Safety Handbook*. **Again, if you are in an emergency call 911.** If you are not in an emergency situation, you can contact the Red Cross to learn more information about CPR and First Aid.)

Dealing with the Sun

Protecting your children from the sun is very important. This is your responsibility. We know from personal experience how easy it is for a child to get sunburned. This is one area where you cannot be too protective.

A Short Story from Mike: "My family and I were on vacation in Florida, and we went to Myakka State Park. We wanted to take a boat ride to see alligators in the wild. We used sunscreen and wore hats to keep us safe from the sun. The kids were fine, however my right forearm, which was outside the boat, got sun poisoning. A sunburn can ruin the most beautiful day."

How to protect your child from the sun. Ask your doctor about the best precautions you can take, and follow your doctor's advice.

1. Avoid direct sunlight between 10 AM and 2 PM, when it is the most dangerous.
2. Make sure your child wears protective clothing when in the sun.
3. Use an umbrella if you're somewhere with no shade.
4. Use at least 45 SPF sunscreen. Make sure the product is waterproof, sweat proof, UVA and UVB effective. Slather your child's hands, neck, feet, ears, and any exposed area.
5. Protect your child's eyes with sunglasses specifically designed to protect her or him from UV rays. With children too young for sunglasses, make sure the child wears a big hat that shades her or his face, or keep her or him in the shade.

Be creative. Children may not want to wear a hat unless it is a fun hat. Also, you can match your sunglasses with theirs so they will want to wear theirs. There's even colorful sunscreen that's fun for kids to wear. Sometimes, you've got to have a gimmick.

Swimming Aids

Coast Guard approved PFDs are great gifts for newborns. Of course, the child won't use it right away, but when the parents are ready to take the child to the water, the parents will have a great tool to keep their child safe.

As your child gets older and more comfortable in the water, you can use swimming aids and put the child in a PFD, so that they can gain confidence in the water while being separate from you. In addition to functioning as water safety devices, PFDs are useful for kids who don't have the dexterity to swim. They help build confidence. The child has fun, and learns to enjoy the water—that's important. **Learn about flotation devices before you use them. This will help keep your child safe.**

Flotation Devices

Flotation Devices fall in two categories: those you hold on to and those that are attached to your body. **Only a personal flotation device/PFD certified by the Coast Guard will keep your child floating and the child's head out of water in an emergency.** No other product will do that.

Even though this is pretty, this is a toy, not a PFD. It's inflatable so it can deflate. It's not Coast Guard approved. It gives you a false sense of security. We insist on a Coast Guard approved PFD.

Swimming aids you hold on to

Only use these devices when in the water supervising your child. Swimming aids are things you hold onto such as kick boards, pull buoys, Styrofoam noodles, and barbell floats. These flotation devices are good for supporting the body in position for learning skills.

They can be useful tools for learning how to swim properly. It can be fun for toddlers if you put the child's armpits over the bar and let the child practice kicking with the barbells supporting her or him. If you are facing the child and walking backward, this will create a draft that will make it easier for the child to move.

Noodles are great for having fun and learning to blow bubbles, as long as there is a supervising adult in the water. You can do many more things with your child including kicking, long Doggy Paddle and back float. However, if he loses the noodle he's going under the water.

Swimming aids that are attached to your body

If, while in the shallow end of the pool, your child is too short to touch the bottom and keep his or her head above water—and you won't be holding your child the whole time—your child should wear a PFD. For infants and toddlers, a PFD is excellent. Be sure to get one that will always keep your child's head above water

If your child hesitates to put on a flotation device, you can demonstrate wearing the belt or jacket first. If the child still doesn't want to, tell your child, "If you don't want to, you don't have to." Try again later.

This is a young child using a swim buoy, which is much more stable than a noodle. It doesn't wobble in the water. The parent and the child can hold it at the same time. Both feel much more secure.

This is a child playing with a noodle. He has a PFD on so it doesn't matter whether he falls in the pool or not. A parent can feel more secure when the jacket is on.

Sometimes kids are fussy when you try to put on the PFD. That's why you have the child wear it at home before he or she ever goes to the pool. We highly recommend that you introduce the PFD at home. You have to be creative about why they should wear it. You can say, "Look what I got you, this beautiful jacket for when we go swimming. And it's also good to wear around the house." You could say this is like what scuba divers wear when they swim. You could compare it to what superheroes have. It's a uniform for the pool, "This is part of your personal swimming suit." "The bright colors will attract fish." "This is a magic jacket." "This is part of your swimming outfit. Older kids play and swim in PFDs. Do you want to try it on?" And you can let the child run around the house in it so your child gets used to it. Do not force anything. If the child is used to it, he or she will put it on easily at the pool or at the beach. If you have an in-ground pool, even with a fence around it, and the child is outside, the child must wear the PFD.

The child is wearing a Coast Guard approved #2 PFD, which is a little less comfortable than a #3 PFD. After he went to the pool with this PFD and did very well, he started wearing a #3 PFD. The advantage of the #2 PFD is that if you become unconscious, the PFD should help turn you face up in the water.

This PFD does not fit the child properly. It's too big. A properly fitting PFD is not up around a child's ears and head. It fits snugly not loosely. It should not restrict the child's head movement. Some people buy a bigger one because kids grow so fast. Having a properly fitting PFD is more important than worrying about having $20 next year. Older children won't wear a poorly fitting jacket. It has to fit or the child won't use it.

This is a #2 PFD. It is specially made for babies up to 25 pounds. It's colorful and children tend to like the colors. It fits properly. It's not over his chin or head, it only goes to the top of his neck. If these two young people let him go, the PFD should help him to lay on his back in the water face up so he can breathe. Also, a parent could say, "Please get him and hand him to me." It's easy to lift the child out of the water because the flap on the back of the PFD has a handle. Another good reason for the PFD is if you've ever tried to hold an infant in the water, as you know, the child is slippery. Parents do drop children. The PFD makes it easier to hold the child.

This is also a #2 PFD for infants. Grandpa's using the handle to lift the toddler out of the water. You could not do this without the PFD.

If a parent has two children in the water, if one has a PFD on, she can handle the other one easily knowing that the child with the PFD will be safe.

If the parents are on deck and lose sight of their child, and they look for their daughter in the pool, if the daughter does not have on her pink PFD puddle jumper, they can easily panic, because they can't find her in the crowd. The PFD keeps the child safer, and the parents more relaxed.

This is a father praising his daughter. This is her first time with the PFD in the water, and she was afraid to put it on. He's saying, "Good job with the PFD. You're very brave. You're doing very well." Remember, we always praise our children for anything that they try.

Inflatable arm bands are a very good tool to build confidence and to practice readiness skills, but they are dangerous. They should only be worn when your child is accompanied by adult supervision. Do not rely on these as a baby sitter. They slip off very easily, especially when your child jumps in the water. A child will build up false confidence with these and believe they are safe when they are not.

These "floaties" or "water wings" can be a useful tool. As your child becomes more confident, you can let a little air out of the floaties, and see how they do.

If you use floaties, teach your child how to jump in with your child's fingers locked together so that the child keeps the floaties on his or her arms. See the section on "jumping in" for more information. You have to watch your child at all times if your child is wearing floaties. There are some floaties that say "WSI approved." They are made of fabric. Even if they are WSI approved, they are still unsafe. The safest PFDs say "Coast Guard Approved."

These are what floaties look like. We do not recommend using them as swimming aids because they slip off so easily.

On the left is a child wearing floaties. On the right is a child in a PFD. Floaties can slide right off your arms when you enter the water or when you're in the water. A Coast Guard approved PFD cannot slide off.

The girl on the left is wearing floaties, so for safety reasons, she must jump in with her fingers interlaced and locked together. Otherwise, the floaties come off. The child on the right is wearing a Coast Guard approved PFD and can jump in with her hands apart. Most of the time, when children jump in, they let go of holding their hands. So the PFD is a better choice than floaties.

Waist bands. Waist bands are made of one piece or several pieces of Styrofoam on a belt that goes around your child's waist. This gives your child more buoyancy in the water and helps support her or him. They also build false confidence and could lead to tragedy if used without supervision. A flotation belt will not keep your child's head out of the water.

With proper supervision, these devices can help with the learning process. They remove the child's fear and allow your child to get used to his or her own buoyancy. By removing the fear, they help the child learn the skill.

The flotation belt is also NOT a PFD. When your child wears a flotation belt, watch your child "like a hawk."

Explain to your child, "This is a buoyancy belt. It will help hold you up." As the child gets more confidence in his own buoyancy, you can remove the squares of foam on the flotation belt, or cut some of the foam off.

This is a buoyancy belt that children wear to help teach swimming. It gives the child extra buoyancy for support. You can remove one floating square at a time, as the child becomes more confident in the water. This is not a PFD, it's just a teaching device.

This is another buoyancy device to aid in teaching. You can't change the buoyancy on this type of device. This is not a PFD.

This is another type of swimming device to help to learn to swim. It's also good for buoyancy, but again it is not a Coast Guard approved PFD. There is also a flotation device on the back of the child. It's held on with elastic.

Yes, we can swim!

Swim fins and paddles: These are for advanced swimmers who already have all the basic skills. Do not give your child swim fins or paddles.

Dangerous Devices or "Toys"

Blown-up animals, rafts, or tubes are among the most dangerous devices your child can use in the water. They give your child a false sense of security. They also give you a false sense of security. With all inflatables, personal supervision is necessary at all times. Your child may want to use these toys and jump in the water without you. The toys are colorful and seem to be so much fun. They should be kept out of reach of all children. **The only safe swimming aid is a properly fitting Coast Guard approved PFD.**

PFDs/Life Jackets

"No buoyant device of any kind has ever been a sure guarantee against drowning. PFD's provide BUOYANCY to support or 'float' the wearer, but vigilance and safety-sense PLUS wearing a good buoyant device are the surest protections. For maximum safety, select the proper size and adjust it to a snug fit."

— The Stearns Company, which manufactures PFDs

All PFDs must be tested after you buy them, to make sure the PFD works on your child to keep his or her head above water, to make sure your child knows how it feels in the water, and so the child knows how to move his or her arms and legs in the water with a PFD. This way there are no surprises if the child falls in the water while wearing the jacket.

Get your child into the habit of wearing a PFD. When you're teaching your child, bring the PFD; and after you teach skills, put the PFD on the child and play with letting the child float. That gives him or her the confidence not to hold on to you all the time. Little by little, as time goes on, if your child gets skilled at swimming with the PFD, you can take it off. But this is where you MUST supervise.

If you live near water, if the pool is in your back yard, or if the water you customarily swim in is cold, get your child used to wearing a PFD.

If you get a child used to wearing a PFD, the child will wear it. It gives the child safety and you confidence. When you're teaching your child to swim, you can take the PFD off and teach swimming skills. But put it back on when you're not teaching.

Get a proper PFD, one that rights the child when he or she falls in. As of publication, these are the standards, but bear in mind, they may change. **A United States Coast Guard approved, Type II (near shore) PFD is good for anyone from an infant to up to someone who weighs 50 pounds** (they are also made up to adult sizes—they're on boats and airplanes). If for any reason your child becomes unconscious in the water or falls in, this type of PFD should flip the child over so the child can breathe. PFDs also help keep people warm. They make the child easy to spot. They're not that bulky. They have a handle on top so you can reach over the side of the boat and just pick the child out of the water if the child falls in.

A U.S. Coast Guard approved, Type III (flotation aid) jacket is for people who weigh 50 pounds and more. It's a general PFD that is also used for boating and sports. It's the most comfortable jacket to wear, but it will not turn your face up in the water so you can breathe. It also does not have a handle. This is made for non-swimmers and swimmers. This jacket is for any child that weighs more than 50 pounds, as of this writing. Please, you must check this for yourself when you purchase your PFD.

The best parents in the world can't watch their children every second. Having your child wear a PFD lets you relax a little. If you're in the ocean and a wave hits, your child gets pulled under, and in a PFD, he or she will pop right back up. If you're in a river and the current takes the child, you know the child will be on the surface if the child is wearing a PFD and you can see her or him. If you're in a lake where you can't see the bottom, and for some reason your child goes under, the PFD brings the child quickly to the surface. PFDs are also good in a crowd. Have you ever tried to pick out your kids on a crowded beach? They mix in with all the other kids. Every second, you think your kid is lost. You know what that does to your heart, "Where is she? Where is he? Oh, there they are!" If you're going to a pool party, and you put the well-fitting Coast Guard approved PFD on for the day, the chances are much better that there will be no drowning incident. If someone asks you an interesting question, you don't have to answer it while scanning the crowd like the searchlight on a prison tower. If a child wearing a PFD is saved once, it's worth every penny.

Caps, Goggles and Earplugs

Caps. Some pools have a rule that you must wear a bathing cap. A cap can keep the hair out of your child's face. Also, if it's made out of rubber or silicone it will keep your child's head warmer because of the barrier between the child's head and the water. Your child may not want to wear a cap. That's OK as long as the facility doesn't require caps. Caps do not keep water out of your child's ears.

Goggles. We encourage parents to teach their children without either parent or child wearing goggles. It's good for children to get used to blinking water out of their eyes when their heads come out of the water. And parents have to set a good example. When Mike teaches, even if a child regularly wears goggles that fit and work properly, at least once Mike teaches the child to go underwater, do an exercise (like counting how many fingers he's holding up), and then the child has to come up and blink the water out of his or her eyes without rubbing with his or her hands. This way, if a child's goggles come off when jumping in or swimming, the child will know the skill and won't panic.

If you're learning to swim or teaching your child, we suggest you try to do it without goggles first. Until your child learns to swim and needs goggles to swim straight because his or her head is in the water, or unless your child has a problem in the water, goggles may delay the learning process and be more of a problem.

Ear Plugs. Before using earplugs we recommend you consult a physician. Your child may not need them. After your child gets his or her ears or head wet, be aware if they are running a temperature or pulling on the ears, this may be a signal that water is a problem for the child. Again, consult with your doctor.

Children's Pool Parties

Children's pool parties can be dangerous situations for children who cannot swim or are unfamiliar with the water. This includes parties in plastic wading pools, backyard pools, public pools that can be rented, or parties at a lake or a beach.

Most places have a lifeguard or a supervising adult, which may be sufficient to prevent a drowning but not a near drowning. A near drowning could cause your child to fear water and experience trauma for a long time.

Mike recently witnessed a pool party in a local public pool. Because the pool was rented for an event, an extra lifeguard was hired. There were no set rules for parents to enter the water with their child. Many parents were not sure if they could enter the water or the parents were afraid of the water. Their children's safety was left to the responsibility of the facility.

Some children brought toy flotation devices into the water that they slipped out of very easily. Because they were not tall enough to stand in the pool, when the devices slipped off, they would begin to panic. There were many incidents of this nature. The two lifeguards were overwhelmed by the number of children who needed assistance.

Remember when you send your child to a pool party, if you are not going to be there, it is still your responsibility to make sure your child is safe. **If your child cannot swim, he or she should be wearing a #2 or #3 Coast Guard approved PFD, and should know better than to take it off.** With this PFD, unless someone holds the child under, he or she should remain on the surface of the water.

Pool parties that are not attended by parents have been known to get out of hand. The children get excited and run. They do not follow the rules. They forget the water is over their heads and they jump in. Parents get a false sense of security because there are lifeguards. The best protection for your child is for you to actively oversee his or her water activities, and have the child wear a PFD at all times. If your child will not wear a PFD, you should either not allow the child to attend, or attend the party to supervise your child.

If your child is at a neighbor's pool, that is often more dangerous because there is no lifeguard present.

What to do if your child gets scared. You want to try to gently desensitize her or him. Move the body and change the mind, in the same environment. For example, with a small child, we suggest going back in the water with your child and holding her or him. Take the child to another place where you do something fun. For younger children, six months to three years old, who are afraid of water, the best way to remove that fear is with fun. You can use a toy, hold her or him close to you in the water and spin, move up and down and sing. As the child gets older, you can have her or him sit on a noodle like it's a horse (pretending it's a horsey ride). A ping-pong ball is a great thing in the pool. You can blow on it. You can throw it. It fits in a kid's hand. It's light. Be imaginative. Children love all kinds of games. When they're having fun, they forget the fear.

If your child is old enough to understand—sometimes four or five years old is old enough—explain to the child why he or she got scared. Then tell the child how not to have that happen again. For instance, if someone pushed the child in the pool or someone dunked the child, and the child went under and got scared, help her or him put on a PFD. Then explain that if he or she had a PFD on and got pushed in, they would come up and be able to breathe. Show the child this in a gradual way.

A. Have the child sit on the side of the pool with a PFD on. Then lift the child in the pool and don't let his or her head get wet. Then take your hands away from the PFD for a moment so the child can feel the buoyancy of the PFD.

B. Then, have the child stand on the side of the pool with toes over the edge, and say, "Bend your knees and jump, and I promise your face won't go in the water." Catch the child when he or she jumps in the pool, and place him or her in water up to the chin. Give positive feedback like, "Wonderful job. You're the best jumper I've ever seen." Then, while your child is still in the water, tell the child to blow some bubbles.

C. Then say, "This time you're going to jump in and your face will go in and you should blow some bubbles. I'll be right here to catch you. When your face goes in the water, you're going to blow bubbles." When your child jumps, catch the child, but let his or her mouth submerge and support the PFD, bringing the child up out of the water. If the child acts surprised or scared, say "You did such a wonderful job. Did you see how well the PFD works?"

Sources

American Red Cross Community Safety (1995) St. Louis, MO: Mosby Lifeline.

American Red Cross Water Safety Handbook (2004) Yardley, PA: Stay Well.

American Red Cross Water Safety Instructor's Manual (2004) Yardley, PA: Stay Well.

American Red Cross Swimming and Water Safety (2004) Yardley, PA: Stay Well.

American Red Cross Teaching Aquatic Skills (1992) St. Louis, MO: Mosby Year Book.

American Red Cross Safety Training for Swim Coaches (1996) St. Louis, MO: Mosby Lifeline.

American Red Cross 'Til Help Arrives (1993) Yardley, PA: Stay Well.

Bruya, Lawrence D. and Langendorfer, Stephen J. (1995) *Aquatic Readiness: Developing Water Competence in Young Children*, Champaign, IL.: Human Kinetics.

Cesari, Judy; Gage, Ross; King, Meredith; Maclean, Jenni; Zancanaro, Julie; Ure, Christine; White, Nell (2001) *Austswim Teaching Infant and Preschool Aquatics, Water Experiences the Australian Way.* Champaign, IL: Human Kinetics.

Harmer, John; Kilpatrick, John; Lowden, Sari; Maclean, Jenni; Marks, Kirk; Meaney, Peter; Richter, Ken; Tulberg, Julie; White, David (2001) *Teaching Swimming and Water Safety The Australian Way.* Champaign, IL: Human Kinetics.

Katz, Dr. Jane (1993) *Swimming for Total Fitness, A complete program for swimming stronger, faster, and better.* New York: Broadway Books.

Katz, Dr. Jane (2002) *Updated Swimming for Total Fitness, A Progressive Aerobic Program.* New York: Broadway Books.

Laughlin, Terry (2001) *Swimming Made Easy The Total Immersion way for any swimmer to achieve fluency, ease and speed in any stroke.* New Paltz, NY: Swimwear.

Leonard, Jr. Kim and Stew with Shapiro, Dr. Lawrence E. (2002) *Stewie the Duck Learns to Swim: A Child's First Guide to Water Safety*. Norwalk, CT: Kimberly Press.

Longfellow's Whales Tales, Water Habits Are Learned Early K-6 Water Safety Education Packet (1989) The American National Red Cross.

Longfellow's Whales Tales Water Habits Are Learned Early K-6 Water Safety Education Video (1995) The American National Red Cross.

LSA Productions (1988) *The Reasons People Drown*. 3 Boulder Brae Lane, Larchmont, NY 10538-1105. (914) 834-9536. http://www.pia-enterprises.com

Spinal Cord Injury Information Network. http://www.spinalcord.uab.edu

Stearns Splash Zone Coloring Book and Size Chart (2000) St. Cloud, MN: Stearns Inc. (Comes with a life vest.)

Tarapinian, Steve (1996) *The Essential Swimmer*. Guilford, CT: The Lyons Press.

Waddles in the Deep, American Red Cross Learn-to-Swim Levels 3 and 4. (2004) Yardley, PA: StayWell.

Waddles Presents Aquacktic Safety (1992) St. Louis, Missouri: Mosby-Year Book, Inc.

Williams, Rozanne Lanczak (2005) *The Swim Lesson*. Huntington Beach, CA: Creative Teaching Press.

INDEX

CPSIA information can be obtained at www.ICGtesting.com
Printed in the USA
LVOW05s1431240615

443695LV00038B/260/P